초등

Grammar
Inside

Student Book
Answer Key

3

Chapter 01 — 조동사

Unit 01 조동사 can

CHECK UP p.9

A
1. jump
2. can
3. be
4. is able to

B
1. ~해도 된다
2. ~할 수 있다
3. ~할 수 있다
4. ~해도 된다
5. ~할 수 있다
6. ~해도 된다

해석
1. 너는 지금 무언가를 말해도 된다.
2. Joe는 세 가지 언어를 말할 수 있다.
3. 그들은 피아노를 잘 칠 수 있다.
4. 그녀는 수업 후에 화장실에 가도 된다.
5. 고양이들은 나무를 오를 수 있다.
6. 너는 이 티셔츠를 입어봐도 된다.

Unit 02 조동사 may, must

CHECK UP p.11

A
1. ⓐ
2. ⓑ
3. ⓐ
4. ⓑ
5. ⓐ
6. ⓑ

B
1. have to
2. must
3. has to
4. call
5. be
6. meet
7. has to

LET'S PRACTICE 1 p.12

A
1. 쓸 수 있다
2. 고칠 수 있다
3. 먹어도 된다
4. 날 수 있다
5. 사용해도 된다
6. 켜도 된다

해석
1. 나는 영어로 편지를 쓸 수 있다.
2. 그는 이 기계를 고칠 수 있다.
3. 너는 지금 점심을 먹어도 된다.
4. 독수리들은 매우 빨리 날 수 있다.
5. 너는 지금 이 마이크를 사용해도 된다.
6. 너는 오후 네 시에 TV를 켜도 된다.

B
1. O
2. X
3. X
4. O
5. X

LET'S PRACTICE 2 p.13

A
1. ⓐ
2. ⓑ
3. ⓑ
4. ⓐ
5. ⓐ

B
1. must follow
2. must eat
3. may be
4. may come
5. have to

STEP UP 1 p.14

A
1. can
2. must
3. may
4. can
5. may
6. can
7. must
8. can
9. must
10. may

B
1. O
2. O
3. X
4. O
5. X
6. O
7. X
8. O
9. O
10. O

STEP UP 2 p.16

A
1. can help Tom
2. may eat salad
3. has to send an email
4. must wait
5. are able to see
6. can wear
7. is able to bake
8. may color
9. must carry
10. can ride

B
1. may[can] have
2. may be
3. must fly
4. may[can] save
5. must repair
6. can walk

STEP UP 3 p.18

A
1. may[can] sit here
2. can[is able to] play the trumpet
3. must[have to] recycle newspaper
4. can[am able to] make pasta
5. may[can] stay here
6. may know each other
7. may be sunny today
8. must[has to] practice hard
9. may[can] bring your friend tomorrow
10. must[have to] get water from the soil

B
1. I can sing pop songs.
2. Amanda may live in India.
3. You must go outside now.
4. My son is able to do his homework alone.
5. She has to change her clothes.
6. He may have a problem with his knee.
7. I must solve the quiz.
8. They are able to speak Korean.

9. There may be some doughnuts in the box.
10. You have to wash your hands now.

STEP UP 4 p.20

A
1. Willy can open his present.
2. Pigs can dig in the ground.
3. You must turn on the light.
4. Josh may be from Japan.
5. Luna has to keep my secret.
6. My sister can count to ten.
7. You may drink a milkshake.
8. She may find treasure.
9. I must finish this job.
10. You may have this wallet.

B
1. My trainer may be sick today.
2. I am able to eat spicy food.
3. You may bring your camera.
4. She may be able to remember my idea.
5. We are able to win the game.
6. He has to go home now.
7. My teacher is able to sing very well.
8. The story may sound familiar.
9. You can change its color.
10. You must sit next to me.

LEVEL UP p.22

A
1. may be sunny   2. can write, letter
3. must meet online   4. is able to lift
5. may[can] drink, milkshake
6. have to wash

B
1. can make pasta
2. may be late
3. may[can] wear my hat
4. must recycle newspaper
5. has to save   6. may[can] stay here
7. are able to run   8. may be, figure skater
9. must go outside   10. may come, school
11. are able to see   12. can[may] bring your

Unit 03   조동사의 부정문

CHECK UP p.25

A   1. ⓐ   2. ⓑ   3. ⓐ   4. ⓑ   5. ⓐ

해석 1 너는 여기서 자전거를 타서는 안 된다.
2 너는 여기서 수영하면 안 된다.
3 너는 여기에 주차해서는 안 된다.
4 너는 여기에 쓰레기를 버려서는 안 된다.
5 너는 여기서 음식을 먹어서는 안 된다.

B   1. climb   2. is not able to
3. doesn't have to   4. must not
5. work   6. may not

Unit 04   조동사의 의문문

CHECK UP p.27

A   1. ⓑ   2. ⓐ   3. ⓐ   4. ⓑ   5. ⓑ   6. ⓐ

B   1. ⓑ   2. ⓒ   3. ⓔ   4. ⓐ   5. ⓓ

LET'S PRACTICE 1 p.28

A   1. ⓑ   2. ⓑ   3. ⓐ   4. ⓑ   5. ⓑ   6. ⓑ   7. ⓐ

B
1. can't smell   2. may not take
3. mustn't bring
4. doesn't have to attend
5. isn't able to speak   6. don't have to find

LET'S PRACTICE 2 p.29

A
1. May I   2. Can you   3. Does Nancy
4. Must I   5. Can they

B
1. I can't   2. you may   3. you can
4. they do   5. we don't have to

STEP UP 1 p.30

A
1. isn't able to   2. mustn't
3. Can you turn on   4. doesn't have to
5. Does he have to   6. Can she play
7. can't sleep   8. may not be
9. Must we feed   10. May I ride

B
1. can't[cannot] make
2. doesn't have to go
3. may not like
4. must not take off
5. aren't able to play

C
1. Must, call   2. Can, send
3. Can, go   4. May, talk to

A
1. can't[cannot] cross 2. Do, have to set
3. Can Sarah catch 4. don't have to record
5. Can I move 6. Must I wait
7. may not read 8. May we follow
9. may not be 10. isn't able to teach

B
1. must[may] not take off
2. may not be
3. Can you speak 4. May[Can] I drink
5. can't push 6. doesn't have to work
7. have to take 8. Must she attend

A
1. don't have to meet
2. Can, turn down, I can
3. may not rain
4. Do, have to water, you do
5. can't[cannot] drive
6. May, see, Yes, you

B
1. Do I have to fix
2. She doesn't have to
3. My daughters cannot watch
4. Can you pass
5. You must not 6. Must we sweep
7. The coffee may not 8. Are you able to
9. You may not 10. May I invite

A
1. She isn't able to walk her dog now.
2. He may not be an artist.
3. You can't drink something here.
4. It may not be sunny today.
5. Jessica can't write letters in Japanese.
6. Minsu doesn't have to go to the airport.
7. You may not sit on the floor.
8. I don't have to pack my bag today.
9. We mustn't move the trash can.
10. This machine isn't able to clean the air.

B
1. Must I go to the library?
2. Can she understand the movie?
3. Does Willy have to help his mom?
4. May she touch the screen?
5. Do they have to wear uniforms?
6. Can Olivia play the game with us?
7. Must he clean the classroom after school?

8. May he stay here for today?
9. Is she able to write her name?
10. Can the students sing a song in the classroom?

A
1. must[may] not drive
2. Must we feed, must
3. Can you pick up, can
4. can't[cannot] cross
5. doesn't have to attend
6. May I ride, Yes

B
1. Can you pass
2. Must I clean
3. You must[may] not travel
4. Does, have to help
5. doesn't have to work
6. Do I have to set
7. Can, send
8. You can't[cannot] run
9. I can't[cannot] smell
10. may not be
11. We aren't able to play

Chapter 01 REVIEW TEST p.40

1. ⓓ 2. ⓑ 3. ⓒ 4. ⓐ 5. ③ 6. ② 7. ②
8. ③ 9. ④ 10. ④ 11. ① 12. ③ 13. ④
14. ① 15. are not able to live 16. Do I have to make a reservation 17. (1) must (2) can (3) may not

1 '의무'를 나타낸다.
2 '허락'을 나타낸다.
3 '추측'을 나타낸다.
4 '능력'을 나타낸다.
5 ③ Can[May] I ~?: 제가 ~해도 될까요? (허락)
6 ② '불가능'을 나타내는 be not able to는 cannot으로 바꿔 쓸 수 있다.
7 ② '금지'를 나타내는 표현이 와야 하므로 '~할 필요가 없다'라 는 의미의 don't have to는 적절하지 않다.
8 ③ 뒤에 도와달라고 요청하는 말이 있으므로 가방을 옮길 수 없다는 '불가능'을 나타내는 cannot이 적절하다.
9 ④ '의무'를 나타내는 have to의 의문문: Do[Does] + 주어 + have to + 동사원형 ~?
10 ① is able to dance → are able to dance ② may are → may be ③ has to study → have to study

11 ② don't have to clean → doesn't have to clean ③ Can your dog swims → Can your dog swim ④ must not playing → must not play

12 ①②④ ~해도 된다 (허락), ③ ~할 수 있다 (능력)

13 ④ 문맥상 첫 번째 빈칸에는 '금지'를 나타내는 must not이 적절하고, 두 번째 빈칸에는 '추측'을 나타내는 may가 적절하다.

14 ① Are you able speak Spanish? → Are you able to speak Spanish?

15 '불가능'을 나타내는 cannot은 be not able to와 바꿔 쓸 수 있다.

16 Do I have to + 동사원형 ~?: 제가 ~해야 하나요?

17 (1) ~해야 한다 (의무) (2) ~해도 된다 (허락) (3) ~해서는 안 된다 (금지)

Chapter 02   일반동사의 과거형

Unit 01   일반동사의 과거형 (1)

CHECK UP   p.47

A   moved, hated, dropped, hugged, cooked, wanted, enjoyed, liked, dried, hurried, loved, failed

B
1. studied 2. listens 3. talked
4. cleaned 5. invited 6. exercise
7. planned

Unit 02   일반동사의 과거형 (2)

CHECK UP   p.49

A
1. came 2. brought 3. gave 4. forgot
5. bought 6. threw 7. paid 8. sang
9. drew 10. sat 11. left 12. taught

B
1. swam 2. chose 3. drink 4. made

LET'S PRACTICE 1   p.50

A
1. worked 2. hated 3. cooked
4. enjoyed 5. walked 6. passed
7. dropped 8. cried 9. dried
10. planned 11. invited 12. washed
13. jumped 14. stopped

B
1. cooked 2. visited 3. moved
4. started 5. listened 6. cleaned

LET'S PRACTICE 2   p.51

A
1. forgot 2. spoke 3. chose 4. hid
5. threw 6. flew 7. built 8. rode
9. brought 10. put 11. hurt 12. ran
13. had 14. made

B
1. X 2. O 3. X 4. X 5. O 6. X

STEP UP 1   p.52

A
1. played 2. hit 3. found 4. wrote
5. danced 6. dropped 7. met
8. forgot 9. watched 10. studied
11. rode 12. went

B
1. lived 2. O 3. O 4. went
5. rained 6. O 7. O 8. cried
9. came 10. drank

STEP UP 2   p.54

A
1. eat, ate 2. studied, studies
3. gets, got 4. reads, read
5. lived, live 6. do, did

B
1. waited 2. bought 3. planted
4. called 5. flew 6. rode 7. won
8. hid 9. felt

STEP UP 3   p.56

A
1. My sister hated rainy days.
2. Jake wanted to be a baseball player.
3. The baby slept for 10 hours.
4. I took Jisu to a movie.
5. My brother drank a lot of soda.
6. Steve made pizza for his family.
7. The boys dried their wet clothes.
8. The students enjoyed the field trip.
9. The girl hugged her teddy bear.
10. We went to the library.

B
1. rode a horse 2. ate a hamburger
3. brushed her teeth 4. bought new shoes
5. cooked this steak 6. came, birthday party

STEP UP 4
p.58

A
1. It snowed a lot last month.
2. We planted flowers in the spring.
3. I bought a backpack for my trip.
4. I cut my finger yesterday.
5. Jim met her at the party last year.
6. She dropped the plate on the floor.
7. He found his wallet at the subway station.
8. She took her daughter to the dentist.
9. The man drove the car too fast.
10. My son broke the vase.

B
1. I wrote a Christmas card.
2. She made a red skirt.
3. He learned Japanese last year.
4. They lived in the city.
5. He hurt his leg.
6. She invented a new machine.
7. I put the plate on the table.
8. She studied math yesterday.
9. I watched an action movie last week.
10. He heard the loud noise a minute ago.

LEVEL UP
p.60

A
1. put, on the table
2. He drove, car
3. ate[had], for dinner
4. We did, last weekend
5. called, last night
6. We planted flowers

B
1. cooked, for breakfast
2. cleaned, an hour
3. Birds flew, south
4. studied math yesterday
5. hugged, teddy bear
6. rode, roller coaster
7. visited his grandparents
8. made pizza, family
9. found your doll
10. fell from
11. waited for me
12. cut my finger

Unit 03   일반동사 과거형의 부정문

CHECK UP
p.63

A 1. V 2. X 3. V 4. V 5. X 6. V 7. V

B 1. didn't 2. didn't 3. brush 4. didn't
5. drink 6. didn't 7. doesn't

Unit 04   일반동사 과거형의 의문문

CHECK UP
p.65

A 1. ⓑ 2. ⓐ 3. ⓑ 4. ⓐ 5. ⓑ

B 1. did 2. No 3. drink, didn't 4. Did, Yes

LET'S PRACTICE 1
p.66

A 1. didn't 2. don't 3. doesn't
4. didn't 5. didn't 6. didn't

B 1. O 2. X 3. X 4. O 5. X 6. O

LET'S PRACTICE 2
p.67

A 1. ⓒ 2. ⓓ 3. ⓑ 4. ⓐ 5. ⓔ

B 1. did 2. didn't 3. does 4. didn't
5. did 6. don't

STEP UP 1
p.68

A
1. didn't write   2. didn't run
3. Did, lose   4. Did, eat
5. didn't know   6. Did, take
7. didn't wear   8. Did, buy
9. didn't forget   10. didn't answer
11. Did, win   12. Did, listen

B
1. didn't 2. arrive 3. O 4. did
5. didn't 6. O 7. did 8. doesn't
9. O 10. Did

STEP UP 2
p.70

A
1. didn't miss   2. find
3. lock   4. didn't pass
5. didn't travel   6. Did he move

7. didn't sell   **8.** bring

9. didn't understand   **10.** Did Mia walk

B   **1.** Did, ride   **2.** didn't do

3. didn't eat, ate   **4.** Did, play, didn't

5. Did, go, did   **6.** didn't drink, drank

STEP UP 3   p.72

A   **1.** didn't go   **2.** didn't understand

3. didn't wake   **4.** didn't read

5. didn't buy

B   **1.** Did, enjoy   **2.** Did, bring

3. Did, visit   **4.** Did, lose

5. Did, lock

C   **1.** Mom didn't bake, Did Mom bake

2. The basketball game didn't end, Did the basketball game end

3. She didn't buy a coat, Did she buy a coat

4. They didn't hear the noise, Did they hear the noise

5. You didn't get a present, Did you get a present

6. He didn't forget, Did he forget

7. Dave didn't hurt his leg, Did Dave hurt his leg

STEP UP 4   p.74

A   **1.** Did she find her puppy?

2. My sister didn't wash her hands.

3. Did Dan travel to Taiwan?

4. I didn't take her to a new restaurant.

5. The runner didn't finish the race.

6. Did her headphones work well?

7. Did Noah write this novel?

8. Janet didn't wear a blue skirt.

9. Did Mia sell her car?

10. Sam didn't eat bread for breakfast.

B   **1.** She didn't work at a restaurant.

2. Did they go to school?

3. I didn't open the window.

4. Did he cook this soup?

5. Did she fix her car?

6. I didn't go shopping last weekend.

7. Did you watch a comedy movie yesterday?

8. We didn't wait for the bus.

9. I didn't sleep on the sofa last night.

---

10. Did you brush your teeth?

LEVEL UP   p.76

A   **1.** Did, walk her dog

2. Did, work well, didn't

3. didn't go to bed

4. students didn't understand

5. didn't eat[have], breakfast

6. Did, win, last year

B   **1.** Did he fix

2. didn't go camping

3. didn't wait for me

4. Did you and Jane have

5. Did, buy, new car

6. They didn't forget

7. Did they arrive

8. didn't work, last year

9. cars didn't move

10. Did, bark at you

11. baseball game didn't end

12. Did, your office

Chapter 02 REVIEW TEST   p.78

1. played   **2.** gets   **3.** had   **4.** ④   **5.** ①

6. ③   **7.** ④   **8.** ③   **9.** ①   **10.** ②   **11.** ②

12. ④   **13.** (1) Ms. Jones taught science at a middle school. (2) I didn't lose my passport at the airport.   **14.** Daniel wore a white shirt

15. (1) Do → Did (2) watch → watched (3) understood → understand

1   과거를 나타내는 말(an hour ago)이 있으므로 과거시제로 써야 한다. (play - played)

2   반복되는 습관을 나타내므로 현재시제로 써야 한다.

3   과거를 나타내는 말(yesterday)이 있으므로 과거시제로 써야 한다. (have - had)

4   ④ find - found

5   ① plan - planned

6   ③ 과거를 나타내는 말(three days ago)이 있으므로 과거시제로 써야 한다. (catch - caught)

7   ④ 내가 했다는 말이 이어지므로 부정의 대답이 알맞고, 질문이 과거형이므로 did를 이용해 답해야 한다.

8   ③ 일반동사 과거형의 부정문: 주어 + didn't + 동사원형

9   ②③④ did[Did], ① Do

10   ② 일반동사 과거형의 의문문: Did + 주어 + 동사원형 ~?, 두 번째 문장은 과거를 나타내는 말(last Sunday)이 있으므로 과거시제로 써야 한다.

11 ① arrive → arrived ③ snow → snowed ④ hurted → hurt

12 ① turned → turn ② wrote → write ③ don't → didn't

13 (1) teach의 과거형은 taught이다. (2) 일반동사 과거형의 부정문: 주어 + didn't + 동사원형

14 wear의 과거형은 wore이다.

15 지난 주말에 있었던 일에 대한 대화이므로 동사를 과거시제로 써야 한다.

실전 Test 01회

p.82

1. ④ **2.** ③ **3.** ④ **4.** ③ **5.** ② **6.** ③ **7.** ②
8. ③ **9.** ④ **10.** ② **11.** ③ **12.** ② **13.** ③
14. ① **15.** ④ **16.** ② **17.** ① **18.** ④
19. (1) Does she have to wear a helmet? (2) Daddy made salad for us. **20.** is not able to finish
21. Henry didn't drink milk **22.** met, studied, ate

1 ④ enjoy - enjoyed

2 ③ sit - sat

3 ④ 하이킹을 갔다는 말이 이어지므로 부정의 대답이 알맞고, 질문이 과거형이므로 did를 이용해 답해야 한다.

4 ③ 과거를 나타내는 말(last weekend)이 있으므로 과거시제를 써야 한다.

5 ② 비밀번호를 잊어버려서 이메일을 확인할 수 없으므로 cannot이 적절하다.

6 ③ may: ~해도 된다

7 ② 거리가 안전하지 않다고 했으므로 불가능이나 금지를 나타내는 표현이 들어가야 한다. don't have to는 '~할 필요가 없다'라는 의미이다.

8 ③ 과거를 나타내는 말(last night)이 있으므로 과거시제만 쓸 수 있다.

9 ④ must ride not → must not ride

10 ② 일반동사 과거형의 부정문: 주어 + didn't + 동사원형 (didn't won → didn't win)

11 ③ 일반동사 과거형의 의문문: Did + 주어 + 동사원형 ~?

12 ①③④ ~해도 된다 (허락), ② ~할 수 있다 (능력)

13 ③ 조동사의 의문문은 「조동사 + 주어 + 동사원형 ~?」의 형태이므로 첫 번째 문장에는 동사원형인 see가 들어가고, have to의 의문문은 일반동사의 의문문 형태로 쓰므로 Does가 들어가야 한다.

14 ① but의 앞 문장은 반복되는 습관을 나타내므로 현재시제, 뒤의 문장은 어제의 일이므로 과거시제로 쓴다.

15 ① beginned → began ② come → came ③ meeted → met

16 ② played → play

17 ① Is he able to bakes → Is he able to bake

18 ④ B가 A의 요청에 응하는 상황이므로 you can이 아니라 I can이 되어야 한다.

19 (1) 의무를 나타내는 have to의 의문문: Does she have to + 동사원형 ~? (2) make의 과거형은 made이다.

20 불가능의 의미를 갖는 cannot이므로 be not able to와 바꿔 쓸 수 있다.

21 일반동사 과거형의 부정문: 주어 + didn't + 동사원형

22 과거를 나타내는 일이므로 일반동사의 과거형을 쓴다.

Chapter 03 명령문

Unit 01 긍정 명령문

CHECK UP
p.89

A **1.** X **2.** V **3.** V **4.** X **5.** V **6.** V **7.** X

해석 **1** 너는 문을 잠근다.
2 네 손을 씻어라.
3 여기서 나가라.
4 그들은 파티에 갔다.
5 우리 집에 와주세요.
6 네 친구들과 음식을 나눠라.
7 그는 많은 물을 마신다.

B **1.** Look **2.** Tell **3.** have **4.** Turn
5. be **6.** Please give **7.** Throw
8. your hand, please

Unit 02 부정 명령문

CHECK UP
p.91

A **1.** ⓑ **2.** ⓐ **3.** ⓐ **4.** ⓐ **5.** ⓑ

B **1.** ⓐ **2.** ⓒ **3.** ⓓ **4.** ⓑ

해석 **1** 여기서 음식을 먹지 마라.
2 여기서 사진을 찍지 마라.
3 여기서 담배를 피우지 마라.
4 여기서 휴대폰을 사용하지 마라.

LET'S PRACTICE 1
p.92

A **1.** O **2.** X **3.** X **4.** O **5.** X **6.** O

B **1.** Cross **2.** remember **3.** Eat **4.** Do
5. Look **6.** Fill

8 초등 Grammar Inside

LET'S PRACTICE 2 p.93

A
1. Don't look   2. worry   3. swim
4. Don't talk   5. stay   6. Don't
7. Never speak

B
1. Don't forget   2. Don't sing
3. Never run   4. don't pick
5. Don't be   6. Never open

STEP UP 1 p.94

A
1. Watch   2. Don't push
3. Leave   4. Don't waste
5. Paint   6. Wear
7. Don't skip   8. return
9. Don't press   10. Don't mix
11. don't ride   12. Spend

B
1. Take   2. Check
3. Don't be   4. Put
5. Don't bother   6. Don't prepare
7. Take out   8. Don't drink
9. Bring   10. Don't forget

STEP UP 2 p.96

A
1. Don't climb up   2. Turn right
3. Don't pick   4. Don't swim
5. Save   6. Wear

B
1. Don't erase   2. Don't go
3. Be   4. Watch out
5. Don't touch   6. Don't mess up
7. Take   8. Plant
9. Don't ask

STEP UP 3 p.98

A
1. Don't run here.
2. Don't hide your report card.
3. Don't be selfish.
4. Don't ask me about Jenny.
5. Don't lock the door.
6. Don't be a lazy student.
7. Don't remove the stickers, please.
8. Please don't open your eyes.
9. Don't prepare for the performance.
10. Don't sing on the stage.

B
1. Wear this pink dress.
2. Don't play the violin at night.
3. Never dive here.
4. Pick these peaches.
5. Be polite to the customers.
6. Never send her a letter.
7. Don't cut in line.
8. Clean your office.
9. Don't be nervous.
10. Remember my birthday.

STEP UP 4 p.100

A
1. Watch this movie with your girlfriend.
2. Don't mix the salad and the dressing.
3. Pack your backpack now.
4. Please don't play baseball here.
5. Return my book by tomorrow.
6. Never fight with your friends.
7. Turn off your cell phone.
8. Don't[Never] use my hair dryer.
9. Please listen to me.
10. Never be late for the class again.

B
1. Write your name here.
2. Bring your tickets.
3. Don't be a liar.
4. Get enough sleep.
5. Don't save the file.
6. Don't cross the bridge.
7. Put two eggs in the soup.
8. Study hard for the exam.
9. Watch out for the snakes in the grass.
10. Don't take this medicine.

LEVEL UP p.102

A
1. Don't walk   2. Wear, pink dress
3. Don't touch   4. Feel, fresh air
5. Turn off, cell phone   6. don't play

B
1. Don't worry, problem
2. Leave here, tomorrow
3. open your eyes
4. Don't talk[speak], slowly
5. Put onions, bowl
6. Don't press, button
7. Share, food, friends

8. Pack your backpack

9. Don't play, violin

10. Don't mess up

11. Pass, sugar, please

12. Don't bother, sister

Chapter 03 REVIEW TEST
p.104

1. Don't ride **2.** Please save **3.** Be **4.** ②
5. ① **6.** ② **7.** ③ **8.** ③ **9.** ④ **10.** ①
11. ③ **12.** ④ **13.** Bring your lunch box.
14. Don't take pictures in the museum.
15. Clean, Eat, Don't[Never] play

1 부정 명령문: Don't[Never] + 동사원형 ~
2 please는 명령문의 앞이나 뒤에 쓴다.
3 명령문은 동사원형으로 시작한다.
4 ② 부정 명령문: Don't[Never] + 동사원형 ~
5 ① 명령문은 동사원형으로 시작한다.
6 ② 명령문은 동사원형으로 시작한다. (Brings → Bring)
7 ③ 부정 명령문: Don't + 동사원형 ~ (is → be)
8 ③ 명령문은 동사원형으로 시작한다.
9 ④ 부정 명령문: Don't[Never] + 동사원형 ~ (Tell never → Never tell)
10 ① 첫 번째 문장은 문맥상 '~하지 마라'라는 의미가 되어야 하므로 Don't이 적절하고, 두 번째 문장은 명령문이므로 동사원형으로 시작한다.
11 ③ 명령문은 동사원형으로 시작하므로 raise가 적절하다. 두 번째 문장은 문맥상 '~하지 마라'라는 의미가 되어야 하므로 Don't be 또는 Never be가 적절하다.
12 ④ 명령문은 동사원형으로 시작한다. (Does → Do)
13 명령문은 동사원형으로 시작한다.
14 부정 명령문: Don't[Never] + 동사원형 ~
15 명령문은 동사원형으로 시작하고, 부정 명령문은 「Don't[Never] + 동사원형 ~」의 형태로 쓴다.

Chapter **04** 제안문

Unit 01 제안문 (1)

CHECK UP
p.111

A **1.** X **2.** V **3.** V **4.** X **5.** V **6.** V

B **1.** study **2.** make **3.** be **4.** not eat
5. Let's not **6.** listen **7.** not

Unit 02 제안문 (2)

CHECK UP
p.113

A **1.** ⓐ **2.** ⓑ **3.** ⓐ **4.** ⓑ

B **1.** wearing **2.** go **3.** send **4.** eating
5. meet **6.** play

LET'S PRACTICE 1
p.114

A **1.** ⓑ **2.** ⓐ **3.** ⓑ **4.** ⓐ **5.** ⓐ **6.** ⓑ

B **1.** Let's not **2.** Let's **3.** Let's
4. Let's **5.** Let's not

LET'S PRACTICE 2
p.115

A **1.** O **2.** X **3.** X **4.** O **5.** X **6.** O

B **1.** ⓑ, ⓒ **2.** ⓐ, ⓑ **3.** ⓐ, ⓒ **4.** ⓑ, ⓒ

해석 1 ⓑ 나와 수업을 듣는 게 어때?
　 ⓒ 나와 식탁을 차리는 게 어때?
2 ⓐ 너 사실을 말하는 게 어때?
　 ⓑ 너 여행을 계획하는 게 어때?
3 ⓐ 우리 이곳을 떠날래?
　 ⓒ 우리 TV를 볼래?
4 ⓑ 노래를 부르는 게 어때?
　 ⓒ Tina를 위해 인형은 어때?

STEP UP 1
p.116

A **1.** Let's play **2.** Let's clean
3. Let's not ring **4.** Let's not drive
5. Let's take **6.** Let's not throw
7. Let's feed **8.** Let's not go
9. Let's not change **10.** Let's print

B **1.** enjoy **2.** drink
3. watching **4.** collect
5. about **6.** reading
7. do **8.** buy
9. Let's not **10.** don't

STEP UP 2　p.118

A
1. Let's turn off
2. don't, go fishing
3. we play outside
4. not ride
5. about curry
6. about drinking tea

B
1. Let's not see
2. we swim
3. Let's not talk
4. about ordering
5. don't we walk
6. don't you dance
7. Let's have
8. about waiting
9. about wearing
10. Shall, meet

STEP UP 3　p.120

A
1. How about cleaning
2. Why don't you turn on
3. Why don't we eat our food
4. Let's leave
5. Shall we go
6. What about going
7. Let's make
8. How about staying
9. Why don't you wear
10. Shall we make

B
1. Let's not be late.
2. How about going there by subway?
3. Shall we travel to Paris?
4. Let's get on the train.
5. How about cleaning the bathroom?
6. Shall we eat bagels for breakfast?
7. Why don't we invite Tom to the party?
8. Why don't you come back next week?
9. Let's not bother the animals.
10. What about trying on the boots?

STEP UP 4　p.122

A
1. Let's not talk about it.
2. Why don't you buy a new cap?
3. Shall we go to the museum?
4. How about traveling to Busan?
5. Let's drink green tea.
6. Why don't we sell those shoes?
7. Let's not touch the window.
8. Shall we study together?
9. Why don't you bring your cat?
10. What about planting trees today?

B
1. Let's help that old man.
2. What about watering the garden?

3. Why don't we take care of your brother?
4. Shall we order soda?
5. Let's meet at the station.
6. Let's not pick the flowers.
7. Why don't you buy a new wallet?
8. Shall we go to the movies?
9. How about playing baseball outside?
10. Let's not call our teacher.

LEVEL UP　p.124

A
1. Let's go
2. How[What], bringing
3. Shall, take
4. Let's not throw
5. Why don't, check
6. about watering

B
1. Shall, go
2. about a doll
3. Why don't, take
4. about reading
5. Let's clean
6. Why don't, tell
7. Let's not pick
8. Why, we invite
9. Shall we swim
10. How[What], going
11. Let's not take
12. Let's meet

Chapter 04 REVIEW TEST　p.126

1. take　**2.** ordering　**3.** go　**4.** not waste
5. don't you　**6.** ②　**7.** ①　**8.** ①　**9.** ②　**10.** ②
11. ③　**12.** ①　**13.** ②　**14.** ④　**15.** Let's not
play computer games.　**16.** Why don't we take
a walk　**17.** (1) Shall we go out (2) Let's make a
snowman (3) How about wearing gloves

1　Let's 제안문에서 Let's 뒤에는 동사원형이 온다.
2　How about 뒤에는 명사나 '-ing'가 온다.
3　Shall we 뒤에는 동사원형이 온다.
4　Let's not + 동사원형 ~: ~하지 말자
5　Why don't you + 동사원형 ~?: 너 ~하는 게 어때?
6　② Let's 제안문의 부정은 Let's not으로 나타낸다.
7　① Why don't we 뒤에는 동사원형이 온다.
8　① 빈칸 뒤에 동사원형이 있으므로 뒤에 명사나 '-ing'가 와야
　　하는 How about은 적절하지 않다.
9　② What about 뒤에는 명사나 '-ing'가 와야 하므로 동사원형
　　은 들어갈 수 없다.
10　② Shall we + 동사원형 ~?: 우리 ~할래?
11　③ Why don't you 뒤에는 동사원형이 온다.
12　① Why don't you와 Let's 뒤에는 동사원형이 온다.
13　② Let's think about not → Let's not think about
14　④ 파스타를 만들자는 제안에 동의한 후에 파스타를 좋아하지
　　않는다고 말하는 것은 어색하다.
15　Let's not + 동사원형 ~: ~하지 말자
16　Why don't we + 동사원형 ~?: 우리 ~하는 게 어때?

17 (1) Shall we + 동사원형 ~?: 우리 ~할래? (2) Let's + 동사원형 ~: ~하자 (3) How about + 명사 / -ing ~?: ~하는 게 어때?

실전 Test 02회
p.130

1. ① **2.** ④ **3.** ① **4.** ③ **5.** ③ **6.** ② **7.** ④
8. ② **9.** ① **10.** ③ **11.** ② **12.** ④ **13.** ②
14. ③ **15.** ② **16.** ① **17.** ③ **18.** ②
19. (1) Don't eat the brownies on the table.
(2) Why don't we watch the sunset at the beach?
20. How about eating a piece of cake?
21. Let's not worry about him. **22.** Shall we swim, Let's not swim

1 ① 부정 명령문: Don't[Never] + 동사원형 ~
2 ④ Let's 제안문에서 Let's 뒤에는 동사원형이 온다.
3 ① Why don't you 뒤에는 동사원형이 온다.
4 ③ 문맥상 '~하지 마라'라는 의미가 되어야 하므로 Don't이 적절하다.
5 ③ 명령문은 동사원형으로 시작한다.
6 ② Why don't we + 동사원형 ~?: 우리 ~하는 게 어때?
7 ④ 부정 명령문: Don't + 동사원형 ~ (is → be)
8 ② How about 뒤에는 명사나 '-ing'가 와야 하므로 동사원형은 들어갈 수 없다.
9 ① Let's 뒤에는 동사원형이 오고, 부정 명령문은 「Don't + 동사원형 ~」이다.
10 ③ Please are → Please be
11 ② Let's take not → Let's not take
12 ④ Why don't you 뒤에는 동사원형이 온다.
13 ② Let's not + 동사원형 ~: ~하지 말자
14 ③ 부정 명령문: Don't[Never] + 동사원형 ~, What about 뒤에는 명사나 '-ing'가 온다.
15 ② How about 뒤에는 명사나 '-ing'가 오고, Why don't you 뒤에는 동사원형이 온다.
16 ① Shall we 뒤에는 동사원형이 온다. (drinking → drink)
17 ③ Let's not + 동사원형 ~: ~하지 말자 (plays → play)
18 ② 공포영화를 보자는 제안에 동의한 후에 공포영화를 좋아하지 않는다고 말하는 것은 어색하다.
19 (1) 부정 명령문: Don't + 동사원형 ~
    (2) Why don't we 뒤에는 동사원형이 온다.
20 How about + 명사 / -ing ~?: ~하는 게 어때?
21 Let's not + 동사원형 ~: ~하지 말자
22 Shall we + 동사원형 ~?: 우리 ~할래?
    Let's not + 동사원형 ~: ~하지 말자

총괄평가 01회

1. ⑤ **2.** ④ **3.** ③ **4.** ② **5.** ④ **6.** ① **7.** ④
8. ③ **9.** ⑤ **10.** ② **11.** ④ **12.** ③ **13.** ③
14. ④ **15.** ⑤ **16.** Don't listen to music loudly.
17. worked → works, start → started
18. We don't have to wait for James.
19. Let's not give up hope. **20.** Are you able to solve this problem?

총괄평가 02회

1. ③ **2.** ⑤ **3.** ⑤ **4.** ③ **5.** ② **6.** ② **7.** ②
8. ④ **9.** ③ **10.** ② **11.** ③ **12.** ④ **13.** ⑤
14. ② **15.** ⑤ **16.** Did the milk smell bad, it did
17. Why don't we buy a new car?
18. He didn't[did not] wash the dishes
19. have to → has to **20.** Don't be rude to your parents.

초등
Grammar
Inside

3

7. is able to keep   8. can park
9. has to change   10. are able to climb

Unit 01 - 02

WORD PRACTICE 2   p.4

A   1. microphone   2. scooter   3. marathon
    4. language   5. count   6. recycle

B   1. lift   2. figure skater   3. safely
    4. familiar   5. repair

C

g	p	c	l	l	d	w	e	r	q
r	c	o	l	o	r	o	s	d	w
o	j	p	s	y	u	w	e	i	l
u	h	e	r	k	r	a	u	g	e
n	g	r	e	s	t	r	o	o	m
d	i	a	b	p	l	n	u	p	l
b	g	l	d	h	e	d	l	e	y
s	a	n	d	c	a	s	t	l	e

    1. color   2. opera   3. restroom
    4. sandcastle   5. dig   6. ground

GRAMMAR PRACTICE 1   p.6

A   1. 점프할 수 있다   2. 따라야 한다
    3. 고칠 수 있다   4. 될지도 모른다
    5. 들어올릴 수 있다   6. 절약해야 한다
    7. 먹어야 한다   8. 잡을 수 있다
    9. 운전할 수 있다   10. 머물러도 된다
    11. 훈련시켜야 한다   12. 타도 된다

B   1. am able to   2. like   3. have to   4. can
    5. be   6. must   7. paint   8. can   9. wear
    10. to control   11. has to   12. can

GRAMMAR PRACTICE 2   p.8

A   1. can   2. may   3. must   4. may
    5. can   6. must   7. can   8. may
    9. must   10. can

B   1. are able to speak   2. may go
    3. must tell   4. are able to swim
    5. have to wash   6. can use

GRAMMAR PRACTICE 3   p.10

A   1. Danny can bake cupcakes.
    2. You may have this umbrella.
    3. They must recycle newspaper.
    4. She may be a figure skater.
    5. We have to carry those dishes.
    6. It may be windy today.
    7. You can turn off the light.
    8. Joe can speak three languages.
    9. She has to wait for the train.
    10. You can bring your sunglasses.

B   1. You may save the file.
    2. Cats are able to see in the dark.
    3. Luna must keep my secret.
    4. Harry has to see a doctor.
    5. You must be careful.
    6. He is able to arrive by 9:00 a.m.
    7. You can eat salad here.
    8. It may be sunny today.
    9. Plants have to get water from the soil.
    10. Emma can play the trumpet.

GRAMMAR PRACTICE 4   p.12

A   1. can walk   2. You may[can] ride
    3. can come   4. have to learn
    5. may be   6. is able to do
    7. may be   8. He can finish
    9. They have to meet
    10. You can[may] color
    11. You must sit
    12. I can[am able to] do my homework alone.
    13. Children must[have to] learn history.
    14. We may be late.
    15. She can[is able to] finish this job.
    16. You can[may] watch TV here.
    17. There may be some pictures in the box.

WORD PRACTICE 2 p.16

A 1. studio 2. plan 3. litter 4. clue
5. grass 6. passport

B 1. take off 2. favor 3. novel 4. join
5. cross

C

s	p	r	o	m	a	r	e	r	c
s	w	e	e	p	y	a	r	a	l
t	t	b	p	e	k	i	a	j	a
a	n	t	w	s	p	n	s	n	n
t	r	a	s	h	q	b	e	n	d
u	p	w	m	p	n	o	u	o	m
e	m	i	c	r	o	w	a	v	e
u	b	p	n	e	w	y	l	e	t

1. statue 2. erase 3. sweep
4. microwave 5. trash 6. bend

GRAMMAR PRACTICE 1 p.18

A 1. ⓑ 2. ⓐ 3. ⓑ 4. ⓑ 5. ⓐ 6. ⓐ

B 1. isn't able to bake 2. mustn't travel
3. can't sleep 4. doesn't have to see
5. may not be

C 1. Can you 2. May I
3. Can she 4. Do I
5. Must Jack

D 1. they can't 2. you may not
3. I can 4. you must
5. she doesn't have to

GRAMMAR PRACTICE 2 p.20

A 1. He may not be
2. Can I drink
3. Must she attend
4. You don't have to record
5. We aren't able to play
6. May we follow
7. Are you able to draw
8. You must not drive
9. doesn't have to work
10. Can I skip

B 1. I cannot climb the mountain.

2. Do they have to go home?
3. Can she play chess?
4. You may not talk to those actors.
5. May I throw this away?
6. Must I wait here?
7. There may not be a present in the box.
8. Ken doesn't have to go to the museum.
9. May I invite you to the party?
10. I am not able to walk my dog now.

GRAMMAR PRACTICE 3 p.22

A 1. I can't fix your washing machine.
2. Amy isn't able to speak Vietnamese.
3. We mustn't take a bus.
4. Jack may not be a firefighter.
5. He doesn't have to attend the meeting.
6. You can't go with me.
7. She may not change the plan.
8. You can't park here.
9. They aren't able to move that statue.
10. You mustn't bring your laptop.

B 1. Can Sarah catch a ball?
2. Do I have to fix your microwave?
3. Must we feed the rabbits?
4. Can they play table tennis?
5. May she touch the screen?
6. Does he have to take the test?
7. Can you speak French?
8. Can I cross the street here?
9. Must we sweep the floor?
10. Can I go shopping?

GRAMMAR PRACTICE 4 p.24

A 1. Can I borrow
2. doesn't have to write
3. isn't able to drive
4. Can, students sing
5. Can she understand
6. may not be
7. Must I erase
8. Does Willy have to help
9. Are you able to climb
10. cannot watch TV
11. You may not sit
12. The weather may not be sunny.
13. Do I have to help you?

14. Can they watch TV late at night?

15. I don't have to write an email.

16. She isn't able to drive a bus.

17. Can I borrow your smartphone?

Chapter 02 — 일반동사의 과거형

Unit 01 - 02

WORD PRACTICE 2
p.28

A 1. plant 2. choose 3. break 4. travel
5. dry 6. dentist

B 1. win 2. try 3. machine 4. hide
5. pay

C

1. drop 2. drive 3. exercise
4. cook 5. build 6. draw

GRAMMAR PRACTICE 1
p.30

A 1. bought 2. eat 3. went 4. started
5. listens 6. rained 7. studies 8. drank
9. live 10. read 11. drove 12. do

B 1. did 2. moved 3. began 4. called
5. read 6. visited 7. cleaned 8. invited
9. swam 10. made 11. planned
12. chose

GRAMMAR PRACTICE 2
p.32

A 1. went 2. hit 3. rode 4. O 5. flew
6. O 7. won 8. hid 9. O 10. O
11. slept 12. O

B 1. played 2. lived 3. fell 4. bought
5. cried 6. came 7. found 8. wrote
9. dropped

GRAMMAR PRACTICE 3
p.34

A 1. We traveled to many countries.
2. They cut the paper in half.
3. I felt lonely.
4. We planted flowers in the spring.
5. Megan got up at 7 o'clock.
6. I rode a roller coaster at an amusement park.
7. Anna and Dave lived in Busan.
8. I ate pasta for lunch.
9. She took her daughter to the dentist.
10. The man drove the car too fast.

B 1. Steve made pizza for his family.
2. I took Jisu to a movie yesterday.
3. The students enjoyed the field trip.
4. She met Jim at the park.
5. I put the plate on the table.
6. She invented a new machine.
7. He hurt his leg.
8. I wrote a Christmas card.
9. He learned Japanese last year.
10. She heard the loud noise a minute ago.

GRAMMAR PRACTICE 4
p.36

A 1. snowed 2. I cut
3. She dropped 4. He found
5. broke 6. I bought
7. He studied 8. I read
9. Amy waited 10. I forgot
11. hugged
12. It rained a lot last year.
13. I found my ring on the sofa.
14. He studied math yesterday.
15. My dad hugged me.
16. She forgot his name.
17. Jake dropped his phone on the desk.

WORD PRACTICE 2   p.40

A 1. bake 2. fix 3. furniture
4. headphone 5. lecture 6. coat

B 1. eat out 2. walk 3. lose 4. wear
5. race

C

e	p	r	o	m	a	r	e	r	c
x	r	c	f	k	p	a	s	a	l
a	i	r	p	o	r	t	e	j	o
m	n	o	w	y	p	n	l	n	c
s	l	s	n	e	q	b	a	r	k
a	p	h	m	p	n	o	u	o	m
t	m	i	s	s	o	w	a	v	e
u	b	p	h	o	w	y	l	e	t

1. exam 2. airport 3. miss
4. ship 5. bark 6. lock

GRAMMAR PRACTICE 1   p.42

A 1. didn't 2. Did 3. doesn't 4. Did
5. cook 6. didn't 7. go 8. Did
9. play 10. Did 11. arrive 12. didn't

B 1. Did, fix   2. Did, bake
3. Did, buy   4. Did, play
5. Did, sleep   6. Did, drink

C 1. they didn't[did not] 2. it didn't[did not]
3. she did   4. I didn't[did not]
5. he did

GRAMMAR PRACTICE 2   p.44

A 1. didn't go   2. didn't work
3. watch   4. didn't wait
5. Did   6. didn't end
7. Did   8. didn't move
9. write   10. didn't sleep
11. didn't find   12. Did

B 1. They didn't enjoy, Did they enjoy
2. He didn't lose, Did he lose
3. She didn't fix, Did she fix
4. Sam didn't visit, Did Sam visit
5. Lucy didn't go, Did Lucy go

6. The students didn't understand, Did the
students understand
7. Her headphones didn't work, Did her
headphones work

GRAMMAR PRACTICE 3   p.46

A 1. I didn't miss the train yesterday.
2. She didn't understand my joke.
3. Did the man sell the painting?
4. James didn't travel to Africa.
5. Did the noise wake him up?
6. I didn't know the answer to the question.
7. Did he play hockey?
8. Did Mia walk her dog last week?
9. I didn't go to the sea last weekend.
10. Jason didn't wear a black shirt yesterday.

B 1. Did you eat French toast for breakfast?
2. She didn't buy the book yesterday.
3. I didn't watch a horror movie last night.
4. Did you hear the noise from outside?
5. Dave didn't answer the phone.
6. My brother didn't read comic books.
7. Did the boys take a taxi?
8. Mom didn't bake this cake.
9. Janet didn't wear a blue skirt.
10. Did you hurt your arm yesterday?

GRAMMAR PRACTICE 4   p.48

A 1. didn't buy
2. Did, end
3. Did, sleep
4. runner didn't finish
5. Did the ship arrive
6. We didn't go
7. He didn't pass
8. Did you bring
9. My sister didn't wash
10. Did you lock
11. Did Sam eat
12. Did he open the window?
13. I didn't[did not] buy a new laptop.
14. Did they arrive at the airport?
15. We didn't[did not] go to the café.
16. Did you sleep on the bed?
17. The movie didn't[did not] end at 4 o'clock.

Unit 01 - 02

WORD PRACTICE 2
p.52

A
1. mistake 2. share 3. worry 4. raise
5. customer 6. bother

B
1. order 2. prepare 3. selfish 4. spend
5. smoke

C

s	p	c	f	l	d	r	u	d	e
i	c	o	r	o	w	o	s	p	w
h	a	l	l	w	a	y	u	o	l
a	h	i	o	k	s	a	w	l	e
e	g	z	j	a	t	r	u	i	m
r	i	a	a	h	e	n	k	t	l
b	p	r	e	s	s	d	l	e	y
s	h	d	r	e	b	a	i	n	c

1. hallway 2. lizard 3. waste
4. rude 5. press 6. polite

GRAMMAR PRACTICE 1
p.54

A
1. Wash 2. come 3. Don't 4. Share
5. be 6. Never 7. sing 8. Help 9. take
10. Please call 11. walk 12. Pass

B
1. Bring   2. Go
3. Don't forget   4. Turn down
5. Don't speak   6. Look
7. Don't stay up 8. Feel
9. Don't read   10. Don't climb up

GRAMMAR PRACTICE 2
p.56

A
1. Tell   2. Never[Don't] swim
3. Don't look   4. Don't make
5. be   6. give
7. Don't worry   8. Raise
9. Don't press

B
1. Watch this video.
2. Don't push your friend.

3. Don't waste water.
4. Wear this blue skirt.
5. Don't ride a bike here.
6. Never fight with your friends.
7. Take out your book.
8. Never open the box.
9. Turn off your cell phone.
10. Don't mess up your room.

GRAMMAR PRACTICE 3
p.58

A
1. Please remember my name.
2. Don't be a liar.
3. Look at the painting.
4. Eat some healthy food.
5. Don't mix these colors.
6. Watch out for the snakes in the grass.
7. Never run in the hallway.
8. Take a bus over there.
9. Fill in the blanks with the right answers.
10. Please return to your seat.

B
1. Watch this movie with your girlfriend.
2. Don't mix the salad and the dressing.
3. Return my book by tomorrow.
4. Don't use my hair dryer.
5. Don't bother your sister.
6. Pack your backpack now.
7. Don't skip breakfast.
8. Don't pick the apples.
9. Spend some time with your mom.
10. Don't be late.

GRAMMAR PRACTICE 4
p.60

A
1. listen to   2. Never be
3. Do   4. don't play
5. Cross   6. Don't drink
7. Put   8. Bring
9. Take   10. Don't be
11. Don't prepare
12. Don't drink too much coffee.
13. Never cross the street here.
14. Put some pepper in the salad.
15. Bring your coat.
16. Don't be shy.
17. Never be late for the meeting again.

Unit 01 - 02

WORD PRACTICE 2 p.64

A 1. collect 2. forest 3. stamp
     4. seatbelt 5. print 6. doorbell

B 1. water 2. invite 3. board game
     4. loudly 5. slowly

C

s	p	c	l	l	d	w	e	r	q
i	n	o	i	s	e	o	s	o	w
n	a	p	s	t	p	w	e	i	p
a	p	i	r	e	r	h	u	e	l
e	g	c	e	t	r	i	p	o	a
r	i	n	b	d	l	d	u	p	n
b	g	i	o	p	t	e	l	e	t
p	u	c	d	n	q	s	t	l	k

     1. nap 2. noise 3. hide
     4. trip 5. picnic 6. plant

GRAMMAR PRACTICE 1 p.66

A 1. not drink 2. go 3. wearing
     4. Let's not 5. do 6. turn 7. go
     8. Let's not 9. playing 10. we
     11. clean 12. watching

B 1. ⓑ 2. ⓐ 3. ⓑ 4. ⓑ 5. ⓑ 6. ⓑ 7. ⓐ

GRAMMAR PRACTICE 2 p.68

A 1. Why don't you eat out
     2. How about playing
     3. Let's drink
     4. What about reading
     5. Shall we take
     6. Let's invite
     7. Shall we go
     8. What about drinking
     9. Why don't we sell
     10. How about studying

B 1. Let's not touch the window.
     2. What about planting trees today?
     3. Why don't you send an email?
     4. Why don't we turn on the music?
     5. Let's not go into the forest.
     6. How about bringing our dog here?
     7. Shall we swim in the pool?
     8. Let's not talk about the exam.
     9. Let's feed this cat.
     10. Shall we go to the museum?

GRAMMAR PRACTICE 3 p.70

A 1. Let's buy a bottle of water.
     2. What about wearing this sweater?
     3. Let's not eat food in the park.
     4. Why don't you enjoy your vacation?
     5. Let's take an express bus.
     6. Why don't we take a nap?
     7. How about a doll for Tina?
     8. Shall we buy these roses?
     9. What about buying new clothes?
     10. Let's not miss the show.

B 1. How about traveling to Busan?
     2. Why don't we walk slowly?
     3. Let's not throw the ball.
     4. Why don't you plan a trip?
     5. Shall we meet at 7:00 a.m.?
     6. Let's make a sandcastle together.
     7. What about turning on the TV?
     8. Why don't we make pasta?
     9. Let's not drive too fast.
     10. Shall we order soda?

GRAMMAR PRACTICE 4 p.72

A 1. Let's clean
     2. Let's not bother
     3. What about staying
     4. Why don't we go
     5. How about wearing
     6. Shall we eat
     7. Why don't you check
     8. Let's not go
     9. What about trying
     10. Shall we hide
     11. Why don't you come

12. What about wearing a cap?

13. Let's not go to the mall.

14. Let's come back next month.

15. How about eating cereal for breakfast?

16. Shall we drink coffee?

17. Why don't we stay on Jeju-do for a while?

MEMO

MEMO

MEMO

MEMO

초등
Grammar
Inside

Workbook

3

MP3

Ⓐ 다음 단어를 두 번씩 듣고 따라 쓴 후 그 뜻을 쓰세요.

단어	두 번 따라 쓰기		뜻 쓰기
color 색칠하다, 색깔			
scooter 스쿠터			
language 언어			
restroom 화장실			
warm up 준비운동을 하다			
opera 오페라			
schedule 일정			
careful 조심하는			
microphone 마이크			
sandcastle 모래성			
lift 들어올리다			
control 조절하다			
save 절약하다, 저장하다			

단어	두 번 따라 쓰기		뜻 쓰기
rule 규칙			
marathon 마라톤			
solve 풀다, 해결하다			
dark 어둠			
figure skater 피겨 스케이팅 선수			
safely 안전하게			
repair 수리하다			
recycle 재활용하다			
dig 땅을 파다			
ground 땅			
count 세다			
treasure 보물			
familiar 익숙한			

A 주어진 철자의 순서를 바르게 맞추어 우리말 뜻에 해당하는 단어를 쓰세요.

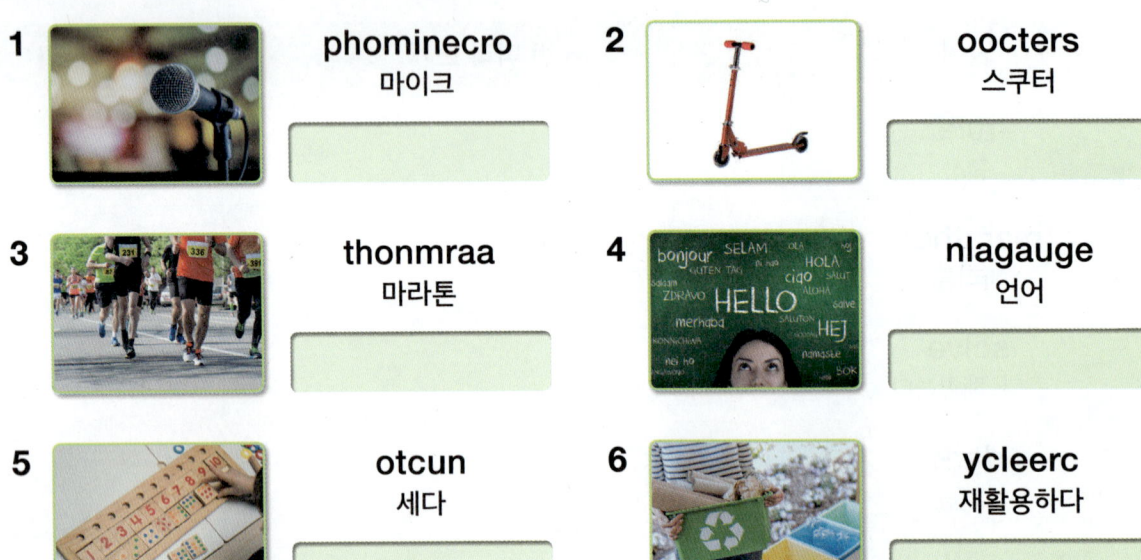

1 phominecro
마이크

2 oocters
스쿠터

3 thonmraa
마라톤

4 nlagauge
언어

5 otcun
세다

6 ycleerc
재활용하다

B 우리말과 같은 뜻이 되도록 보기 에서 알맞은 단어를 골라 쓰세요.

| 보기 | familiar | lift | figure skater | repair | safely |

1 I can _____ this big bag.   나는 이 큰 가방을 들어올릴 수 있다.

2 My mom was a _____ before.   나의 엄마는 전에 피겨 스케이팅 선수셨다.

3 You have to drive _____.   너는 안전하게 운전해야 한다.

4 I'm not _____ with this program.   나는 이 프로그램에 익숙하지 않다.

5 They can _____ this car.   그들은 이 차를 수리할 수 있다.

C 다음 사진에 해당하는 단어를 아래 퍼즐에서 찾아 ○ 표시하고 빈칸에 쓰세요.

g	p	c	l	l	d	w	e	r	q
r	c	o	l	o	r	o	s	d	w
o	j	p	s	y	u	w	e	i	l
u	h	e	r	k	r	a	u	g	e
n	g	r	e	s	t	r	o	o	m
d	i	a	b	p	l	n	u	p	l
b	g	l	d	h	e	d	l	e	y
s	a	n	d	c	a	s	t	l	e

1

색칠하다, 색깔

2

오페라

3

화장실

4

모래성

5

땅을 파다

6

땅

A 밑줄 친 부분의 우리말 뜻을 고르세요.

1 He <u>can jump</u> very high.   (점프할 수 있다 / 점프해도 된다)

2 You <u>must follow</u> some rules.   (따라야 한다 / 따라도 된다)

3 I <u>can fix</u> the computer.   (고칠지도 모른다 / 고칠 수 있다)

4 Nicky <u>may be</u> the winner.   (될지도 모른다 / 되어야 한다)

5 He <u>is able to lift</u> this box.   (들어올려야 한다 / 들어올릴 수 있다)

6 He <u>has to save</u> money.   (절약할 수 있다 / 절약해야 한다)

7 She <u>must eat</u> healthy food.   (먹어도 된다 / 먹어야 한다)

8 I <u>can hold</u> your hand.   (잡아야 한다 / 잡을 수 있다)

9 Lisa <u>is able to drive</u> a car.   (운전할 수 있다 / 운전할 지도 모른다)

10 You <u>may stay</u> here.   (머물러도 된다 / 머물러야 한다)

11 I <u>have to train</u> my dogs.   (훈련시킬 수 있다 / 훈련시켜야 한다)

12 You <u>can ride</u> a scooter here.   (타도 된다 / 타야 한다)

B ( ) 안에서 알맞은 것을 고르세요.

1 I (be able to / am able to) write a letter in English. 나는 영어로 편지를 쓸 수 있다.

2 She may (like / likes) opera. 그녀는 오페라를 좋아할지도 모른다.

3 They (has to / have to) use this dictionary. 그들은 이 사전을 사용해야 한다.

4 You (can / cans) eat lunch now. 너는 지금 점심을 먹어도 된다.

5 It may (be / is) cold outside. 밖은 추울지도 모른다.

6 I (must / has to) buy a new phone. 나는 새 휴대폰을 사야 한다.

7 You may (paint / painted) this wall. 너는 이 벽을 칠해도 된다.

8 Eagles (can / is able to) fly very fast. 독수리들은 매우 빨리 날 수 있다.

9 Betty must (wear / wearing) a jacket. Betty는 재킷을 입어야 한다.

10 You are able (control / to control) your mind. 너는 너의 마음을 조절할 수 있다.

11 He (have to / has to) get an A on the exam. 그는 시험에서 A를 받아야 한다.

12 She (can / be able to) read this map. 그녀는 이 지도를 읽을 수 있다.

A 우리말과 같은 뜻이 되도록 빈칸에 can, may, must 중 알맞은 말을 쓰세요.

1 그들은 모래성을 만들 수 있다.

→ They _____ make a sandcastle.

2 그는 과학자일지도 모른다.

→ He _____ be a scientist.

3 그녀는 일정을 바꿔야 한다.

→ She _____ change the schedule.

4 Linda는 학교에 일찍 올지도 모른다.

→ Linda _____ come to school early.

5 토끼들은 빨리 뛸 수 있다.

→ Rabbits _____ run fast.

6 이 비행기는 안전하게 날아야 한다.

→ This airplane _____ fly safely.

7 그는 이 기계를 고칠 수 있다.

→ He _____ fix this machine.

8 그들은 감기에 걸릴지도 모른다.

→ They _____ catch a cold.

9 우리는 이 컴퓨터를 수리해야 한다.

→ We _____ repair this computer.

10 나는 중국어를 할 수 있다.

→ I _____ speak Chinese.

B 두 문장이 같은 의미가 되도록 빈칸에 알맞은 말을 쓰세요.

1 They can speak Korean.　그들은 한국어를 할 수 있다.

→ They ＿＿＿＿＿ ＿＿＿＿＿ ＿＿＿＿＿ ＿＿＿＿＿

Korean.

2 You can go to the festival today.　너는 오늘 그 축제에 가도 된다.

→ You ＿＿＿＿＿ ＿＿＿＿＿ to the festival today.

3 Fred has to tell me the truth.　Fred는 나에게 진실을 말해야 한다.

→ Fred ＿＿＿＿＿ ＿＿＿＿＿ me the truth.

4 Tim and Larry can swim well.　Tim과 Larry는 수영을 잘 할 수 있다.

→ Tim and Larry ＿＿＿＿＿ ＿＿＿＿＿ ＿＿＿＿＿

＿＿＿＿＿ well.

5 You must wash your hands now.　너는 지금 네 손을 씻어야 한다.

→ You ＿＿＿＿＿ ＿＿＿＿＿ ＿＿＿＿＿ your hands now.

6 You may use this microphone now.　너는 지금 이 마이크를 사용해도 된다.

→ You ＿＿＿＿＿ ＿＿＿＿＿ this microphone now.

7 She can keep a secret.　그녀는 비밀을 지킬 수 있다.

→ She ＿＿＿＿＿ ＿＿＿＿＿ ＿＿＿＿＿ ＿＿＿＿＿ a

secret.

8 You may park here.　너는 여기에 주차해도 된다.

→ You ＿＿＿＿＿ ＿＿＿＿＿ here.

9 She must change her clothes.　그녀는 옷을 갈아입어야 한다.

→ She ＿＿＿＿＿ ＿＿＿＿＿ ＿＿＿＿＿ her clothes.

10 Cats can climb trees.　고양이들은 나무를 올라갈 수 있다.

→ Cats ＿＿＿＿＿ ＿＿＿＿＿ ＿＿＿＿＿ ＿＿＿＿＿

trees.

A 우리말과 같은 뜻이 되도록 주어진 말을 바르게 배열하세요.

1 Danny는 컵케이크를 구울 수 있다. (bake / can / Danny / cupcakes / .)

→ _____

2 너는 이 우산을 가져도 된다. (you / this / have / umbrella / may / .)

→ _____

3 그들은 신문을 재활용해야 한다. (must / they / recycle / newspaper / .)

→ _____

4 그녀는 피겨 스케이팅 선수일지도 모른다. (a figure skater / may / she / be / .)

→ _____

5 우리는 저 접시들을 옮겨야 한다. (those dishes / we / carry / have to / .)

→ _____

6 오늘 바람이 불지도 모른다. (be / it / may / windy / today / .)

→ _____

7 너는 불을 꺼도 된다. (can / you / turn off / the light / .)

→ _____

8 Joe는 세 가지 언어로 말할 수 있다. (can / three languages / speak / Joe / .)

→ _____

9 그녀는 그 기차를 기다려야 한다. (the train / has to / she / wait for / .)

→ _____

10 너는 네 선글라스를 가져와도 된다. (bring / can / sunglasses / you / your / .)

→ _____

B 밑줄 친 부분을 바르게 고쳐 문장을 다시 쓰세요.

1 You <u>mays</u> save the file.   너는 그 파일을 저장해도 된다.

→ _____

2 Cats <u>be able to</u> see in the dark.   고양이들은 어둠 속에서 볼 수 있다.

→ _____

3 Luna must <u>keeps</u> my secret.   Luna는 내 비밀을 지켜야 한다.

→ _____

4 Harry <u>have to</u> see a doctor.   Harry는 병원에 가야 한다.

→ _____

5 You must <u>are</u> careful.   너는 조심해야 한다.

→ _____

6 He <u>be able to</u> arrive by 9:00 a.m.   그는 오전 9시까지 도착할 수 있다.

→ _____

7 You can <u>eating</u> salad here.   너는 여기서 샐러드를 먹어도 된다.

→ _____

8 It may <u>is</u> sunny today.   오늘은 화창할지도 모른다.

→ _____

9 Plants <u>has to</u> get water from the soil.   식물들은 흙에서 물을 얻어야 한다.

→ _____

10 Emma can <u>plays</u> the trumpet.   Emma는 트럼펫을 연주할 수 있다.

→ _____

A 우리말과 같은 뜻이 되도록 주어진 말을 이용하여 문장을 완성하세요.

1 나는 매우 빨리 걸을 수 있다. (walk)

➡ I _____ _____ really fast.

2 너는 여기서 자전거를 타도 된다. (ride)

➡ _____ _____ _____ a bike here.

3 우리의 꿈들은 실현될 수 있다. (come)

➡ Our dreams _____ _____ true.

4 너는 역사를 배워야 한다. (learn)

➡ You _____ _____ _____ history.

5 그 배우는 늦을지도 모른다. (be)

➡ The actor _____ _____ late.

6 내 아들은 혼자 숙제를 할 수 있다. (do)

➡ My son _____ _____ _____ _____
his homework alone.

7 상자 안에 도넛 몇 개가 있을지도 모른다. (be)

➡ There _____ _____ some doughnuts in the box.

8 그는 마라톤을 끝낼 수 있다. (finish)

➡ _____ _____ _____ a marathon.

9 그들은 온라인에서 만나야 한다. (meet)

➡ _____ _____ _____ _____ online.

10 너는 내 그림에 색칠해도 된다. (color)

➡ _____ _____ _____ my picture.

11 너는 내 옆에 앉아야 한다. (sit)

➡ _____ _____ _____ next to me.

12 나는 혼자 숙제를 할 수 있다. (my homework)

➡ _____

13 아이들은 역사를 배워야 한다. (children)

➡ _____

14 우리는 늦을지도 모른다. (be)

➡ _____

15 그녀는 이 일을 끝낼 수 있다. (this job)

➡ _____

16 너는 여기서 TV를 봐도 된다. (watch TV)

➡ _____

17 상자 안에 사진 몇 장이 있을지도 모른다. (some pictures)

➡ _____

MP3

Ⓐ 다음 단어를 두 번씩 듣고 따라 쓴 후 그 뜻을 쓰세요.

단어	두 번 따라 쓰기		뜻 쓰기
grass 잔디, 풀			
throw 던지다			
litter 버리다			
bend 굽히다			
studio 스튜디오			
erase 지우다			
essay 에세이, 수필			
favor 부탁			
join 가입하다			
washing machine 세탁기			
plan 계획			
statue 동상			
attend 참석하다			

단어	두 번 따라 쓰기		뜻 쓰기
clue 단서			
trash 쓰레기			
feed 먹이를 주다			
take off 벗다			
cross 건너다			
record 기록하다			
life jacket 구명조끼			
water 물을 주다			
passport 여권			
microwave 전자레인지			
novel 소설			
sweep 쓸다			
invite 초대하다			

초등 Grammar Inside 4

A 주어진 철자의 순서를 바르게 맞추어 우리말 뜻에 해당하는 단어를 쓰세요.

1 ustiod
스튜디오

2 lnap
계획

3 ttlier
버리다

4 lcue
단서

5 argss
잔디, 풀

6 opatsspr
여권

B 우리말과 같은 뜻이 되도록 보기 에서 알맞은 단어를 골라 쓰세요.

보기   join   take off   novel   favor   cross

1 You must _____ your shoes here.   너는 여기서 너의 신발을 벗어야 한다.

2 Can I ask you a _____?   내가 너에게 부탁 하나 해도 될까?

3 Her new _____ is very popular.   그녀의 새 소설은 인기가 매우 많다.

4 Can I _____ your club?   내가 너희 동아리에 가입해도 될까?

5 We can _____ the street here.   우리는 여기서 길을 건널 수 있다.

C 다음 사진에 해당하는 단어를 아래 퍼즐에서 찾아 ○ 표시하고 빈칸에 쓰세요.

s	p	r	o	m	a	r	e	r	c
s	s	w	e	e	p	y	a	r	a	l
t	t	b	p	e	k	i	a	j	a
a	n	t	w	s	p	n	s	n	n
t	r	a	s	h	q	b	e	n	d
u	p	w	m	p	n	o	u	o	m
e	m	i	c	r	o	w	a	v	e
u	b	p	n	e	w	y	l	e	t

1

동상

2

지우다

3

쓸다

4

전자레인지

5

쓰레기

6

굽히다

A 부정문으로 바꿀 때 not이 들어갈 위치를 고르세요.

1 You ⓐ can ⓑ ride a bike ⓒ here.   너는 여기서 자전거를 타도 된다.

2 She is ⓐ able to ⓑ set ⓒ the schedule.   그녀는 일정을 짤 수 있다.

3 You ⓐ must ⓑ swim ⓒ here.   너는 여기서 수영해야 한다.

4 Your story ⓐ may ⓑ be ⓒ true.   너의 이야기는 사실일지도 모른다.

5 I can ⓐ make ⓑ a robot ⓒ.   나는 로봇을 만들 수 있다.

6 They may ⓐ take ⓑ photos ⓒ here.   그들은 여기서 사진을 찍어도 된다.

B 밑줄 친 부분을 부정형으로 바꿔 쓰세요. (축약형으로 쓰세요.)

1 She is able to bake cookies.   ➔ _____
그녀는 쿠키를 구울 수 있다.

2 You must travel alone.   ➔ _____
너는 혼자 여행해야 한다.

3 I can sleep well.   ➔ _____
나는 잠을 잘 잘 수 있다.

4 Joe has to see a doctor.   ➔ _____
Joe는 병원에 가야 한다.

5 They may be twins.   ➔ _____
그들은 쌍둥이일지도 모른다.

C 보기 에서 알맞은 말을 골라 쓰세요.

> 보기   May I   Must Jack   Can she   Can you   Do I

1 A: _____ do me a favor?   B: Sure, I can.
부탁 하나 들어주겠니?   물론 할 수 있어.

2 A: _____ speak to your brother?   B: No, you may not.
내가 너의 남동생에게 말해도 될까?   아니, 안 돼.

3 A: _____ play the guitar?   B: No, she can't.
그녀는 기타를 칠 수 있니?   아니, 못해.

4 A: _____ have to wear a sweater?   B: Yes, you do.
나는 스웨터를 입어야 하니?   응, 그래.

5 A: _____ join our club?   B: Yes, he must.
Jack이 우리 동아리에 가입해야 하니?   응, 그래.

D 빈칸에 알맞은 말을 써서 대답을 완성하세요.

1 A: Can they make soup for us?   B: No, _____.
그들은 우리를 위해 수프를 만들 수 있니?   아니, 못해.

2 A: May I visit your office?   B: No, _____.
내가 너의 사무실에 방문해도 될까?   아니, 안 돼.

3 A: Can you pick up the trash?   B: Yes, _____.
쓰레기를 주워주겠니?   응, 그래.

4 A: Must I clean the window?   B: Yes, _____.
나는 창문을 청소해야 하니?   응, 그래.

5 A: Does she have to sit here?   B: No, _____.
그녀는 여기에 앉아야 하니?   아니, 그러지 않아도 돼.

A 우리말과 같은 뜻이 되도록 주어진 말을 바르게 배열하세요.

1 그는 배가 고프지 않을지도 모른다. (not / he / may / be)

→ _____ hungry.

2 내가 물 한 잔을 마셔도 될까? (I / can / drink)

→ _____ a glass of water?

3 그녀가 그 파티에 참석해야 하니? (must / attend / she)

→ _____ the party?

4 너는 모든 것을 기록하지 않아도 된다. (record / have to / you / don't)

→ _____ everything.

5 우리는 바이올린을 연주할 수 없다. (able / we / play / aren't / to)

→ _____ the violin.

6 우리가 당신을 따라가도 될까요? (we / may / follow)

→ _____ you?

7 너는 무지개를 그릴 수 있니? (able / to / are / draw / you)

→ _____ a rainbow?

8 너는 여기서 운전하면 안 된다. (not / you / drive / must)

→ _____ here.

9 Jun은 더 이상 일을 할 필요가 없다. (have to / work / doesn't)

→ Jun _____ anymore.

10 내가 오늘의 수업을 빼먹어도 될까? (I / skip / can)

→ _____ today's class?

B 밑줄 친 부분을 바르게 고쳐 문장을 다시 쓰세요.

1 I cannot <u>climbing</u> the mountain.　나는 산을 오를 수 없다.

➡ _____

2 <u>Does</u> they have to go home?　그들은 집에 가야 하니?

➡ _____

3 Can she <u>plays</u> chess?　그녀는 체스를 할 수 있니?

➡ _____

4 You <u>may talk not</u> to those actors.　너는 저 배우들에게 이야기해서는 안 된다.

➡ _____

5 <u>I may</u> throw this away?　내가 이것을 버려도 될까?

➡ _____

6 <u>Musts</u> I wait here?　나는 여기서 기다려야 하니?

➡ _____

7 There <u>not may</u> be a present in the box.　상자 안에 선물이 없을지도 모른다.

➡ _____

8 Ken doesn't <u>has to</u> go to the museum.　Ken은 박물관에 갈 필요가 없다.

➡ _____

9 May I <u>invited</u> you to the party?　제가 당신을 파티에 초대해도 될까요?

➡ _____

10 I <u>be not able to</u> walk my dog now.　나는 지금 나의 개를 산책시킬 수 없다.

➡ _____

A 다음 문장을 부정문으로 바꿔 쓰세요. (축약형으로 쓰세요.)

1 I can fix your washing machine.   나는 너의 세탁기를 고칠 수 있다.

→ _____

2 Amy is able to speak Vietnamese.   Amy는 베트남어를 할 수 있다.

→ _____

3 We must take a bus.   우리는 버스를 타야 한다.

→ _____

4 Jack may be a firefighter.   Jack은 소방관일지도 모른다.

→ _____

5 He has to attend the meeting.   그는 그 회의에 참석해야 한다.

→ _____

6 You can go with me.   너는 나와 함께 가도 된다.

→ _____

7 She may change the plan.   그녀는 계획을 바꿀지도 모른다.

→ _____

8 You can park here.   너는 여기에 주차해도 된다.

→ _____

9 They are able to move that statue.   그들은 저 동상을 옮길 수 있다.

→ _____

10 You must bring your laptop.   너는 너의 노트북 컴퓨터를 가져와야 한다.

→ _____

B 다음 문장을 의문문으로 바꿔 쓰세요.

1 Sarah can catch a ball.   Sarah는 공을 잡을 수 있다.

➡ _____

2 I have to fix your microwave.   나는 너의 전자레인지를 고쳐야 한다.

➡ _____

3 We must feed the rabbits.   우리는 토끼들에게 먹이를 주어야 한다.

➡ _____

4 They can play table tennis.   그들은 탁구를 칠 수 있다.

➡ _____

5 She may touch the screen.   그녀는 화면을 만져도 된다.

➡ _____

6 He has to take the test.   그는 그 시험을 쳐야 한다.

➡ _____

7 You can speak French.   너는 프랑스어를 할 수 있다.

➡ _____

8 I can cross the street here.   나는 여기서 길을 건너도 된다.

➡ _____

9 We must sweep the floor.   우리는 바닥을 쓸어야 한다.

➡ _____

10 I can go shopping.   나는 쇼핑을 가도 된다.

➡ _____

A 우리말과 같은 뜻이 되도록 주어진 말을 이용하여 문장을 완성하세요.

1 내가 너의 펜을 빌려도 될까? (can, borrow)

→ _____ _____ _____ your pen?

2 그녀는 편지를 쓸 필요가 없다. (have to, write)

→ She _____ _____ _____ _____ a
letter.

3 그는 트럭을 운전할 수 없다. (be able to, drive)

→ He _____ _____ _____ _____ a
truck.

4 학생들은 교실에서 노래를 불러도 되니? (can, students, sing)

→ _____ the _____ _____ a song in the
classroom?

5 그녀는 그 영화를 이해할 수 있니? (can, understand)

→ _____ _____ _____ the movie?

6 그 커피는 뜨겁지 않을지도 모른다. (may, be)

→ The coffee _____ _____ _____ hot.

7 내가 칠판을 지워야만 하니? (must, erase)

→ _____ _____ _____ the board?

8 Willy는 그의 엄마를 도와야만 하니? (have to, help)

→ _____ _____ _____ _____
_____ his mom?

9 너는 나무에 오를 수 있니? (be able to, climb)

➡ _____ _____ _____ _____

_____ a tree?

10 내 딸들은 밤늦게 TV를 봐서는 안 된다. (cannot, watch TV)

➡ My daughters _____ _____ _____ late at

night.

11 너는 바닥에 앉아서는 안 된다. (may, sit)

➡ _____ _____ _____ _____ on the

floor.

12 날씨가 화창하지 않을지도 모른다. (the weather, may, be sunny)

➡ _____

13 내가 너를 도와야만 하니? (have to, help)

➡ _____

14 그들은 밤늦게 TV를 볼 수 있니? (can, watch TV, late at night)

➡ _____

15 나는 이메일을 쓸 필요가 없다. (have to, write an email)

➡ _____

16 그녀는 버스를 운전할 수 없다. (be able to, a bus)

➡ _____

17 내가 너의 스마트폰을 빌려도 될까? (can, your smartphone)

➡ _____

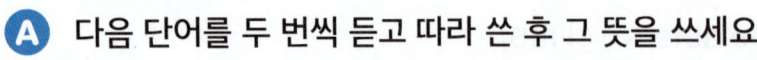 다음 단어를 두 번씩 듣고 따라 쓴 후 그 뜻을 쓰세요.

단어	두 번 따라 쓰기	뜻 쓰기
cook 요리하다		
arrive 도착하다		
try 시도하다		
dry 말리다		
plan 계획하다		
drop 떨어뜨리다		
invent 발명하다		
fail 실패하다		
wedding 결혼식		
exercise 운동하다		
win 이기다		
drive 운전하다		
break 깨다		

단어	두 번 따라 쓰기		뜻 쓰기
hide 숨기다			
draw 그리다			
choose 고르다			
build (건물을) 짓다			
pay 지불하다			
beat 이기다			
hurt 다치게 하다			
password 비밀번호			
travel 여행하다			
plant 심다			
wet 젖은			
dentist 치과			
machine 기계			

A 주어진 철자의 순서를 바르게 맞추어 우리말 뜻에 해당하는 단어를 쓰세요.

1
antlp
심다

2
hscoeo
고르다

3
bkrae
깨다

4
rtvale
여행하다

5
dyr
말리다

6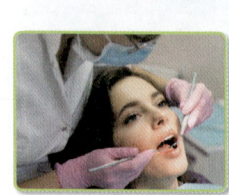
entdtsi
치과

B 우리말과 같은 뜻이 되도록 보기 에서 알맞은 단어를 골라 쓰세요.

보기	hide	try	machine	win	pay

1 We can ＿＿＿＿＿＿＿ the game.　우리는 그 경기에서 이길 수 있다.

2 Always ＿＿＿＿＿＿＿ your best.　항상 최선을 다해라.

3 There is a new ＿＿＿＿＿＿＿ in the factory.　공장 안에 새 기계가 한 대 있다.

4 My brothers often ＿＿＿＿＿＿＿ their toys.　내 남동생들은 자주 장난감들을 숨긴다.

5 You have to ＿＿＿＿＿＿＿ 30 dollars.　너는 30달러를 지불해야 한다.

C 다음 사진에 해당하는 단어를 아래 퍼즐에서 찾아 ○ 표시하고 빈칸에 쓰세요.

s	p	c	l	l	d	w	e	r	e
i	d	r	i	v	e	o	s	o	x
n	r	p	s	y	j	t	e	i	e
a	o	d	r	k	s	a	u	e	r
e	p	r	e	s	r	r	o	o	c
r	i	a	b	p	c	o	o	k	i
b	g	w	b	u	i	l	d	e	s
s	a	y	d	c	m	v	t	n	e

1

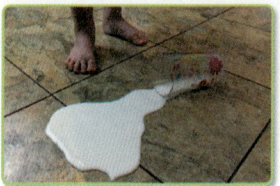

떨어뜨리다

2

운전하다

3

운동하다

4

요리하다

5

(건물을) 짓다

6

그리다

A ( ) 안에서 알맞은 것을 고르세요.

1 She (buied / bought) a new laptop yesterday.   그녀는 어제 새 노트북 컴퓨터를 샀다.

2 I (eat / ate) eggs for breakfast every day.   나는 매일 아침으로 계란을 먹는다.

3 I (goed / went) to bed late last night.   나는 지난밤에 늦게 잠들었다.

4 The movie (started / starts) 10 minutes ago.   영화는 10분 전에 시작했다.

5 She (listens / listened) to music every morning.
그녀는 매일 아침 음악을 듣는다.

6 It (rained / rainned) a lot last Monday.   지난주 월요일에 비가 많이 왔다.

7 He (studies / studied) American history these days.
그는 요즘 미국의 역사를 공부한다.

8 She (drinked / drank) too much coffee yesterday.
그녀는 어제 너무 많은 커피를 마셨다.

9 They (live / lived) in China now.   그들은 지금 중국에 산다.

10 He (read / reads) some novels last week.   그는 지난주에 소설 몇 권을 읽었다.

11 Jake (drived / drove) a car for the first time.   Jake는 처음으로 차를 운전했다.

12 I (do / did) the laundry every Saturday.   나는 토요일마다 빨래를 한다.

B 주어진 단어를 과거형으로 바꾸어 문장을 완성하세요.

1 I _____ my homework last night. (do) 나는 지난밤에 숙제를 했다.

2 We _____ the furniture. (move) 우리는 가구를 옮겼다.

3 The musical _____ 5 minutes late. (begin) 뮤지컬은 5분 늦게 시작했다.

4 I _____ Emily last night. (call) 나는 지난밤에 Emily에게 전화했다.

5 Anna _____ the book last week. (read) Anna는 그 책을 지난주에 읽었다.

6 James _____ his grandparents. (visit) James는 그의 조부모님을 방문했다.

7 I _____ the bathroom an hour ago. (clean)
나는 한 시간 전에 욕실을 청소했다.

8 We _____ her to our wedding. (invite) 우리는 그녀를 우리의 결혼식에 초대했다.

9 The boy _____ in the pool. (swim) 그 소년은 수영장에서 수영했다.

10 I _____ cookies for you. (make) 나는 너를 위해 쿠키들을 만들었다.

11 We _____ our trip to America last year. (plan)
우리는 작년에 미국으로의 여행을 계획했다.

12 She _____ a blue dress. (choose) 그녀는 파란색 원피스를 골랐다.

A 밑줄 친 부분이 맞으면 ◯ 표시하고, 틀리면 바르게 고쳐 쓰세요.

1 Bora <u>goed</u> shopping with her mom. ➜ _____
보라는 그녀의 엄마와 쇼핑을 하러 갔다.

2 The car <u>hitted</u> the wall. ➜ _____
그 차는 벽을 들이받았다.

3 I <u>rided</u> a bike yesterday. ➜ _____
나는 어제 자전거를 탔다.

4 She <u>got up</u> late yesterday. ➜ _____
그녀는 어제 늦게 일어났다.

5 Birds <u>flyed</u> fast to the south. ➜ _____
새들이 남쪽으로 빠르게 날아갔다.

6 I <u>studied</u> Chinese last week. ➜ _____
나는 지난주에 중국어를 공부했다.

7 Our team <u>win</u> the final game. ➜ _____
우리 팀이 결승전에서 이겼다.

8 The girl <u>hided</u> her toy under the bed. ➜ _____
그 소녀는 그녀의 장난감을 침대 아래에 숨겼다.

9 She <u>planted</u> a tree in the garden. ➜ _____
그녀는 정원에 나무를 심었다.

10 I <u>danced</u> with Jim at the party. ➜ _____
나는 파티에서 Jim과 춤을 췄다.

11 The baby <u>sleeped</u> for 10 hours. ➜ _____
그 아기는 10시간 동안 잤다.

12 Jake <u>wanted</u> to be a baseball player. ➜ _____
Jake는 야구 선수가 되기를 원했다.

B 우리말과 같은 뜻이 되도록 보기 에서 알맞은 단어를 골라 과거형으로 바꾸세요.

| 보기 | find | drop | buy | come | cry | play | fall | live | write |

1 나는 친구들과 축구를 했다.

→ I _____ soccer with my friends.

2 우리 가족은 2012년에 미국에 살았다.

→ My family _____ in America in 2012.

3 나뭇잎들이 나무에서 떨어졌다.

→ The leaves _____ from the tree.

4 그는 어제 파란색 모자를 샀다.

→ He _____ a blue hat yesterday.

5 그 아기는 한 시간 동안 울었다.

→ The baby _____ for an hour.

6 Eric은 한 시간 전에 집으로 돌아왔다.

→ Eric _____ back home an hour ago.

7 나는 네 인형을 소파 아래에서 찾았다.

→ I _____ your doll under the sofa.

8 Jim은 그의 선생님께 이메일을 썼다.

→ Jim _____ an email to his teacher.

9 Brad는 컵을 떨어뜨렸다.

→ Brad _____ the cup.

A 다음 문장을 과거시제로 바꿔 쓰세요.

1 We travel to many countries.   우리는 많은 나라들로 여행한다.

➜ _____

2 They cut the paper in half.   그들은 종이를 반으로 자른다.

➜ _____

3 I feel lonely.   나는 외로움을 느낀다.

➜ _____

4 We plant flowers in the spring.   우리는 봄에 꽃들을 심는다.

➜ _____

5 Megan gets up at 7 o'clock.   Megan은 7시에 일어난다.

➜ _____

6 I ride a roller coaster at an amusement park.   나는 놀이공원에서 롤러코스터를 탄다.

➜ _____

7 Anna and Dave live in Busan.   Anna와 Dave는 부산에 산다.

➜ _____

8 I eat pasta for lunch.   나는 점심으로 파스타를 먹는다.

➜ _____

9 She takes her daughter to the dentist.   그녀는 그녀의 딸을 치과에 데리고 간다.

➜ _____

10 The man drives the car too fast.   그 남자는 차를 너무 빨리 운전한다.

➜ _____

B 밑줄 친 부분을 바르게 고쳐 문장을 다시 쓰세요.

1 Steve <u>maked</u> pizza for his family.   Steve는 그의 가족을 위해 피자를 만들었다.

➜ _____

2 I <u>take</u> Jisu to a movie yesterday.   나는 어제 지수를 데리고 영화를 보러 갔다.

➜ _____

3 The students <u>enjoied</u> the field trip.   학생들은 소풍을 즐겼다.

➜ _____

4 She <u>meeted</u> Jim at the park.   그녀는 Jim을 공원에서 만났다.

➜ _____

5 I <u>puted</u> the plate on the table.   나는 접시를 테이블 위에 놓았다.

➜ _____

6 She <u>invent</u> a new machine.   그녀는 새 기계를 발명했다.

➜ _____

7 He <u>hurted</u> his leg.   그는 그의 다리를 다쳤다.

➜ _____

8 I <u>writed</u> a Christmas card.   나는 크리스마스 카드를 썼다.

➜ _____

9 He <u>learns</u> Japanese last year.   그는 작년에 일본어를 배웠다.

➜ _____

10 She <u>heared</u> the loud noise a minute ago.   그녀는 조금 전에 시끄러운 소리를 들었다.

➜ _____

A 우리말과 같은 뜻이 되도록 주어진 말을 이용하여 문장을 완성하세요.

1 지난달에 눈이 많이 내렸다. (snow)

➜ It _____ a lot last month.

2 나는 어제 내 손가락을 베었다. (cut)

➜ _____ _____ my finger yesterday.

3 그녀는 접시를 바닥에 떨어뜨렸다. (drop)

➜ _____ _____ the plate on the floor.

4 그는 그의 지갑을 지하철역에서 찾았다. (find)

➜ _____ _____ his wallet at the subway station.

5 나의 아들이 그 꽃병을 깨뜨렸다. (break)

➜ My son _____ the vase.

6 나는 내 여행을 위해 배낭을 샀다. (buy)

➜ _____ _____ a backpack for my trip.

7 그는 그 당시에 프랑스어를 공부했다. (study)

➜ _____ _____ French at that time.

8 나는 지난달에 책 세 권을 읽었다. (read)

➜ _____ _____ three books last month.

9 Amy는 오랫동안 나를 기다렸다. (wait)

➡ _____ _____ for me for a long time.

10 나는 내 비밀번호를 잊어버렸다. (forget)

➡ _____ _____ my password.

11 그 소녀는 그녀의 곰인형을 안았다. (hug)

➡ The girl _____ her teddy bear.

12 작년에 비가 많이 내렸다. (rain, last year)

➡ _____

13 나는 내 반지를 소파 위에서 찾았다. (my ring, on the sofa)

➡ _____

14 그는 어제 수학을 공부했다. (math, yesterday)

➡ _____

15 나의 아빠는 나를 안으셨다. (my dad)

➡ _____

16 그녀는 그의 이름을 잊어버렸다. (his name)

➡ _____

17 Jake는 그의 핸드폰을 책상 위에 떨어뜨렸다. (his phone, on the desk)

➡ _____

A 다음 단어를 두 번씩 듣고 따라 쓴 후 그 뜻을 쓰세요.

단어	두 번 따라 쓰기		뜻 쓰기
walk 걷다, (동물을) 산책시키다			
brush 빗질을 하다, 이를 닦다			
exam 시험			
airport 공항			
bark (개가) 짖다			
fix 고치다			
eat out 외식하다			
bake 굽다			
work 일하다, 작동하다			
lose 잃어버리다			
wear 입다			
ship 배			
port 항구			

단어	두 번 따라 쓰기		뜻 쓰기
miss 놓치다			
lock 잠그다			
understand 이해하다			
joke 농담			
lecture 강의			
furniture 가구			
coat 코트			
noise 소음			
race 경주			
headphone 헤드폰			

A   주어진 철자의 순서를 바르게 맞추어 우리말 뜻에 해당하는 단어를 쓰세요.

1    abke
굽다

2   xif
고치다

3    tureinfur
가구

4    onedaehph
헤드폰

5    eltcrue
강의

6    oact
코트

B   우리말과 같은 뜻이 되도록 보기 에서 알맞은 단어를 골라 쓰세요.

보기	wear	eat out	walk	lose	race

1 Let's _____ tonight.   오늘 저녁에 외식하자.

2 We _____ our dogs every day.   우리는 매일 우리 개들을 산책시킨다.

3 Did you _____ your passport?   너는 너의 여권을 잃어버렸니?

4 He doesn't _____ glasses.   그는 안경을 쓰지 않는다.

5 Can she win the _____?   그녀가 그 경주에서 이길 수 있을까?

C 다음 사진에 해당하는 단어를 아래 퍼즐에서 찾아 ◯ 표시하고 빈칸에 쓰세요.

e	p	r	o	m	a	r	e	r	c
x	r	c	f	k	p	a	s	a	l
a	i	r	p	o	r	t	e	j	o
m	n	o	w	y	p	n	l	n	c
s	l	s	n	e	q	b	a	r	k
a	p	h	m	p	n	o	u	o	m
t	m	i	s	s	o	w	a	v	e
u	b	p	h	o	w	y	l	e	t

1

시험

2

공항

3

놓치다

4

배

5

(개가) 짖다

6

잠그다

A ( ) 안에서 알맞은 것을 고르세요.

1 I (don't / didn't) go camping last weekend. 나는 지난 주말에 캠핑을 가지 않았다.

2 (Do / Did) you take the exam yesterday? 너는 어제 시험을 봤니?

3 He (doesn't / didn't) have his wallet now. 그는 지금 그의 지갑이 없다.

4 (Does / Did) he call you last night? 그가 지난밤에 네게 전화를 했니?

5 Did she (cook / cooked) food for you? 그녀가 너를 위해 음식을 요리했니?

6 He (doesn't / didn't) visit the doctor yesterday. 그는 어제 병원에 가지 않았다.

7 We didn't (go / went) to Taiwan last year. 우리는 작년에 대만에 가지 않았다.

8 (Does / Did) he win a gold medal last year? 그는 작년에 금메달을 땄니?

9 She didn't (play / played) basketball. 그녀는 농구를 하지 않았다.

10 (Do / Did) you finish your homework? 너는 숙제를 끝냈니?

11 Did they (arrive / arrived) at the airport? 그들은 공항에 도착했니?

12 He (doesn't / didn't) go to bed early last night. 그는 지난밤에 일찍 자지 않았다.

B 주어진 말을 이용하여 과거시제의 의문문을 완성하세요.

1 _____ he _____ the bike? (fix)

그는 자전거를 수리했니?

2 _____ they _____ the cookies? (bake)

그들이 그 쿠키를 구웠니?

3 _____ Amy _____ a birthday cake? (buy)

Amy는 생일 케이크를 샀니?

4 _____ he _____ tennis? (play)

그는 테니스를 쳤니?

5 _____ you _____ well last night? (sleep)

너는 지난밤에 잘 잤니?

6 _____ she _____ orange juice? (drink)

그녀는 오렌지 주스를 마셨니?

C 빈칸에 알맞은 말을 넣어 대화를 완성하세요.

1 A: Did they visit your office?   B: No, _____.

그들이 너의 사무실을 방문했니?   아니, 그렇지 않았어.

2 A: Did your computer work well?   B: No, _____.

너의 컴퓨터는 잘 작동했니?   아니, 그렇지 않았어.

3 A: Did she bring her friend?   B: Yes, _____.

그녀는 그녀의 친구를 데리고 왔니?   응, 그랬어.

4 A: Did you brush your teeth?   B: No, _____.

너는 이를 닦았니?   아니, 그렇지 않았어.

5 A: Did he cook this soup?   B: Yes, _____.

그가 이 수프를 요리했니?   응, 그랬어.

A 밑줄 친 부분을 바르게 고쳐 쓰세요.

1 I <u>don't go</u> shopping last weekend. ➜ _____
나는 지난 주말에 쇼핑을 가지 않았다.

2 She <u>didn't worked</u> at a restaurant. ➜ _____
그녀는 식당에서 일하지 않았다.

3 Did you <u>watched</u> a comedy movie yesterday? ➜ _____
너는 어제 코미디 영화를 봤니?

4 Sam <u>didn't waits</u> for me yesterday. ➜ _____
Sam은 어제 나를 기다리지 않았다.

5 <u>Does</u> she work at a hotel last year? ➜ _____
그녀는 작년에 호텔에서 일했니?

6 The baseball game <u>didn't ended</u> at 8 o'clock. ➜ _____
야구 경기는 8시에 끝나지 않았다.

7 <u>Does</u> Dave hurt his leg in a soccer game? ➜ _____
Dave는 축구 경기에서 그의 다리를 다쳤니?

8 He <u>doesn't moved</u> to Seoul last year. ➜ _____
그는 작년에 서울로 이사하지 않았다.

9 Did Noah <u>wrote</u> this novel? ➜ _____
Noah가 이 소설을 썼니?

10 I <u>don't slept</u> on the sofa last night. ➜ _____
나는 지난밤에 소파에서 잠을 자지 않았다.

11 She <u>didn't found</u> her puppy. ➜ _____
그녀는 그녀의 강아지를 찾지 못했다.

12 <u>Do</u> you exercise yesterday? ➜ _____
너는 어제 운동했니?

B 빈칸에 알맞은 말을 써서 부정문과 의문문을 각각 완성하세요. (부정문은 축약형으로 쓰세요.)

1 They enjoyed the party. 그들은 파티를 즐겼다.

→ _____ the party.

→ _____ the party?

2 He lost his umbrella. 그는 그의 우산을 잃어버렸다.

→ _____ his umbrella.

→ _____ his umbrella?

3 She fixed her car. 그녀는 그녀의 차를 수리했다.

→ _____ her car.

→ _____ her car?

4 Sam visited his grandmother. Sam은 그의 할머니를 방문했다.

→ _____ his grandmother.

→ _____ his grandmother?

5 Lucy went to school yesterday. Lucy는 어제 학교에 갔다.

→ _____ to school yesterday.

→ _____ to school yesterday?

6 The students understood the lecture. 학생들은 그 강의를 이해했다.

→ _____ the lecture.

→ _____ the lecture?

7 Her headphones worked well. 그녀의 헤드폰은 잘 작동했다.

→ _____ well.

→ _____ well?

A 다음 문장을 주어진 지시대로 바꿔 쓰세요. (부정문은 축약형으로 쓰세요.)

1 I missed the train yesterday. (부정문)　나는 어제 기차를 놓쳤다.

→ _____

2 She understood my joke. (부정문)　그녀는 나의 농담을 이해했다.

→ _____

3 The man sold the painting. (의문문)　그 남자는 그 그림을 팔았다.

→ _____

4 James traveled to Africa. (부정문)　James는 아프리카로 여행을 갔다.

→ _____

5 The noise woke him up. (의문문)　그 소음은 그를 깨웠다.

→ _____

6 I knew the answer to the question. (부정문)　나는 그 질문에 대한 답을 알았다.

→ _____

7 He played hockey. (의문문)　그는 하키를 했다.

→ _____

8 Mia walked her dog last week. (의문문)　Mia는 지난주에 그녀의 개를 산책시켰다.

→ _____

9 I went to the sea last weekend. (부정문)　나는 지난 주말에 바다에 갔다.

→ _____

10 Jason wore a black shirt yesterday. (부정문)　Jason은 어제 검정색 셔츠를 입었다.

→ _____

B 밑줄 친 부분을 바르게 고쳐 문장을 다시 쓰세요. (부정문은 축약형으로 쓰세요.)

1 Did you ate French toast for breakfast? 너는 아침으로 프렌치 토스트를 먹었니?

→ _____

2 She doesn't buy the book yesterday. 그녀는 어제 그 책을 사지 않았다.

→ _____

3 I don't watch a horror movie last night. 나는 지난밤에 공포 영화를 보지 않았다.

→ _____

4 Do you heard the noise from outside? 너희는 바깥으로부터의 소음을 들었니?

→ _____

5 Dave didn't answered the phone. Dave는 전화를 받지 않았다.

→ _____

6 My brother not did read comic books. 내 남동생은 만화책들을 읽지 않았다.

→ _____

7 Did the boys took a taxi? 그 소년들은 택시를 탔니?

→ _____

8 Mom didn't baked this cake. 엄마가 이 케이크를 굽지 않으셨다.

→ _____

9 Janet didn't wears a blue skirt. Janet은 파린색 치마를 입지 않았다.

→ _____

10 Do you hurt your arm yesterday? 너는 어제 네 팔을 다쳤니?

→ _____

A 우리말과 같은 뜻이 되도록 주어진 말을 이용하여 문장을 완성하세요.

1 내 부모님은 새 가구를 사지 않으셨다. (buy)

➡ My parents _____ _____ new furniture.

2 농구 경기는 5시에 끝났니? (end)

➡ _____ the basketball game _____ at 5 o'clock?

3 너의 고양이는 바닥에서 잤니? (sleep)

➡ _____ your cat _____ on the floor?

4 그 주자는 경주를 끝내지 않았다. (runner, finish)

➡ The _____ _____ _____ the race.

5 배가 항구에 도착했니? (the ship, arrive)

➡ _____ _____ _____ _____ at the

port?

6 우리는 그 이탈리아 식당에 가지 않았다. (go)

➡ _____ _____ _____ to the Italian restaurant.

7 그는 어제 시험을 통과하지 않았다. (pass)

➡ _____ _____ _____ the test yesterday.

8 너는 너의 우산을 가지고 왔니? (bring)

➡ _____ _____ _____ your umbrella?

9 내 여동생은 손을 씻지 않았다. (my sister, wash)

➡ _____ _____ _____ _____ her

hands.

10 너는 문을 잠갔니? (lock)

➡ _____ _____ _____ the door?

11 Sam은 아침으로 빵을 먹었니? (eat)

➡ _____ _____ _____ bread for breakfast?

12 그가 창문을 열었니? (open, the window)

➡ _____

13 나는 새 노트북 컴퓨터를 사지 않았다. (buy, a new laptop)

➡ _____

14 그들은 공항에 도착했니? (at the airport)

➡ _____

15 우리는 그 카페에 가지 않았다. (the café)

➡ _____

16 너는 침대 위에서 잤니? (on the bed)

➡ _____

17 그 영화는 4시에 끝나지 않았다. (the movie, end, at 4 o'clock)

➡ _____

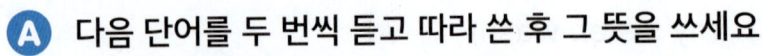

A 다음 단어를 두 번씩 듣고 따라 쓴 후 그 뜻을 쓰세요.

단어	두 번 따라 쓰기		뜻 쓰기
order 주문하다			
share 나누다			
raise 올리다			
rude 무례한			
smoke 담배를 피우다			
straight 똑바로, 곧은			
blank 빈칸			
worry 걱정하다			
mistake 실수			
hallway 복도			
waste 낭비하다			
press 누르다			
spend (시간, 돈을) 쓰다			

단어	두 번 따라 쓰기		뜻 쓰기
bother 괴롭히다			
prepare 준비하다			
corner 모퉁이			
safety glove 안전 장갑			
mess up 어질러 놓다			
watch out 조심하다			
lizard 도마뱀			
report card 성적표			
selfish 이기적인			
remove 제거하다			
performance 공연			
polite 공손한			
customer 고객			

A 주어진 철자의 순서를 바르게 맞추어 우리말 뜻에 해당하는 단어를 쓰세요.

1 　**imtskae**
실수

2 　**hrsea**
나누다

3 　**rwoyr**
걱정하다

4 　**rsiae**
올리다

5 　**tosucrem**
고객

6 　**thober**
괴롭히다

B 우리말과 같은 뜻이 되도록 보기 에서 알맞은 단어를 골라 쓰세요.

| 보기 | smoke | prepare | selfish | order | spend |

1 Can you ＿＿＿＿＿＿ lunch for me?　나를 위해 점심을 주문해 주겠니?

2 We must ＿＿＿＿＿＿ for the class.　우리는 수업을 준비해야 한다.

3 A ＿＿＿＿＿＿ person can lose friends.　이기적인 사람은 친구들을 잃을 수 있다.

4 Don't ＿＿＿＿＿＿ too much money.　돈을 너무 많이 쓰지 마라.

5 Some people ＿＿＿＿＿＿ here.　몇몇 사람들이 여기서 담배를 피운다.

C 다음 사진에 해당하는 단어를 아래 퍼즐에서 찾아 ○ 표시하고 빈칸에 쓰세요.

s	p	c	f	l	d	r	u	d	e
i	c	o	r	o	w	o	s	p	w
h	a	l	l	w	a	y	u	o	l
a	h	i	o	k	s	a	w	l	e
e	g	z	j	a	t	r	u	i	m
r	i	a	a	h	e	n	k	t	l
b	p	r	e	s	s	d	l	e	y
s	h	d	r	e	b	a	i	n	c

1

복도

2

도마뱀

3

낭비하다

4

무례한

5

누르다

6

공손한

A ( ) 안에서 알맞은 것을 고르세요.

1 (Wash / Washing) your hands.   네 손을 씻어라.

2 Please (come / came) to my house.   우리 집에 와주세요.

3 (Not / Don't) start the game.   게임을 시작하지 마라.

4 (Share / Shares) the food with your friends.   네 친구들과 음식을 나눠라.

5 Don't (is / be) sad.   슬퍼하지 마라.

6 (Doesn't / Never) leave me alone.   절대 나를 혼자 남겨두지 마라.

7 Don't (singing / sing) too loud at night.   밤에 너무 크게 노래하지 마라.

8 (Helping / Help) your mom right now.   지금 너의 엄마를 도와라.

9 Don't (take / taking) pictures here.   여기서 사진을 찍지 마라.

10 (Call please / Please call) me back.   제게 다시 전화해주세요.

11 Don't (walk / to walk) your dog here.   여기서 개를 산책시키지 마라.

12 (Pass / Passed) me the sugar, please.   제게 설탕을 건네주세요.

B 다음 문장을 명령문으로 바꿔 쓸 때 빈칸에 알맞은 말을 쓰세요.

1 You bring your toys. 너는 너의 장난감들을 가져온다.

➡ _____ your toys.

2 You go straight two blocks. 너는 두 블록을 직진한다.

➡ _____ straight two blocks.

3 You don't forget their address. 너는 그들의 주소를 잊지 않는다.

➡ _____ their address.

4 You turn down the volume. 너는 볼륨을 줄인다.

➡ _____ the volume.

5 You don't speak during an exam. 너는 시험 중에 말하지 않는다.

➡ _____ during an exam.

6 You look at those buildings. 너는 저 건물들을 본다.

➡ _____ at those buildings.

7 You don't stay up late at night. 너는 밤늦게까지 깨어있지 않는다.

➡ _____ late at night.

8 You feel the fresh air. 너는 신선한 공기를 느낀다.

➡ _____ the fresh air.

9 You don't read this book. 너는 이 책을 읽지 않는다.

➡ _____ this book.

10 You don't climb up the tree. 너는 나무를 오르지 않는다.

➡ _____ the tree.

A 우리말과 같은 뜻이 되도록 보기에서 알맞은 단어를 골라 쓰세요. (필요하면 형태를 바꾸세요.)

보기	press	raise	be	tell	look
	give	swim	make	worry	

1 그녀에게 너의 비밀을 말해줘라.

➜ _____ her your secret.

2 여기에서 절대 수영하지 마세요.

➜ _____ here, please.

3 뒤를 돌아보지 마라.

➜ _____ back.

4 어떤 실수도 하지 마라.

➜ _____ any mistakes.

5 조심하세요.

➜ Please _____ careful.

6 나에게 당신의 주소를 주세요.

➜ Please _____ me your address.

7 그 문제에 대해 걱정하지 마라.

➜ _____ about that problem.

8 손을 들어주세요.

➜ _____ your hand, please.

9 그 버튼을 누르지 마세요.

➜ _____ the button, please.

B 우리말과 같은 뜻이 되도록 주어진 말을 바르게 배열하세요.

1 이 영상을 봐라. (this / watch / video / .)

→ _____

2 네 친구를 밀지 마라. (push / don't / friend / your / .)

→ _____

3 물을 낭비하지 마라. (water / waste / don't / .)

→ _____

4 이 파란색 치마를 입어라. (blue skirt / this / wear / .)

→ _____

5 여기서 자전거를 타지 마라. (a bike / here / ride / don't / .)

→ _____

6 네 친구들과 절대 싸우지 마라. (your / fight with / never / friends / .)

→ _____

7 네 책을 꺼내라. (your / take out / book / .)

→ _____

8 그 상자를 절대 열지 마라. (the box / open / never / .)

→ _____

9 네 휴대폰을 꺼라. (your / turn off / cell phone / .)

→ _____

10 네 방을 어질러 놓지 마라. (your room / don't / mess up / .)

→ _____

A 밑줄 친 부분을 바르게 고쳐 문장을 다시 쓰세요.

1 Please <u>remembers</u> my name.   내 이름을 기억해주세요.

→ _____

2 <u>Don't is</u> a liar.   거짓말쟁이가 되지 마라.

→ _____

3 <u>Looks</u> at the painting.   그림을 봐라.

→ _____

4 <u>To eat</u> some healthy food.   건강한 음식을 좀 먹어라.

→ _____

5 <u>Doesn't mix</u> these colors.   이 색들을 섞지 마라.

→ _____

6 <u>Watching</u> out for the snakes in the grass.   잔디의 뱀들을 조심해라.

→ _____

7 <u>Never not</u> run in the hallway.   복도에서 절대 뛰지 마라.

→ _____

8 <u>Taking</u> a bus over there.   저기 있는 버스를 타라.

→ _____

9 <u>Fills</u> in the blanks with the right answers.   맞는 답들로 빈칸들을 채워라.

→ _____

10 Please <u>returned</u> to your seat.   당신의 자리로 돌아가주세요.

→ _____

B 다음 문장을 주어진 지시대로 바꿔 쓰세요.

1 You watch this movie with your girlfriend. (긍정 명령문)
너는 네 여자친구와 함께 이 영화를 본다.

➡ _____

2 You mix the salad and the dressing. (부정 명령문)   너는 샐러드와 드레싱을 섞는다.

➡ _____

3 You return my book by tomorrow. (긍정 명령문)   너는 내 책을 내일까지 돌려준다.

➡ _____

4 You use my hair dryer. (부정 명령문)   너는 내 헤어드라이어를 사용한다.

➡ _____

5 You bother your sister. (부정 명령문)   너는 너의 여동생을 괴롭힌다.

➡ _____

6 You pack your backpack now. (긍정 명령문)   너는 지금 네 배낭을 싼다.

➡ _____

7 You skip breakfast. (부정 명령문)   너는 아침을 거른다.

➡ _____

8 You pick the apples. (부정 명령문)   너는 사과들을 딴다.

➡ _____

9 You spend some time with your mom. (긍정 명령문)   너는 너의 엄마와 시간을 좀 보낸다.

➡ _____

10 You are late. (부정 명령문)   너는 늦는다.

➡ _____

A 우리말과 같은 뜻이 되도록 주어진 말을 이용하여 문장을 완성하세요.

1 제 말을 들어주세요. (listen to)

→ Please _____ _____ me.

2 절대 수업에 다시 늦지 마라. (never, be)

→ _____ _____ late for the class again.

3 숙제를 먼저 해라. (do)

→ _____ your homework first.

4 여기서 야구를 하지 마세요. (play)

→ Please _____ _____ baseball here.

5 여기서 길을 건너라. (cross)

→ _____ the street here.

6 탄산음료를 너무 많이 마시지 마라. (drink)

→ _____ _____ too much soda.

7 수프에 달걀을 두 개 넣어라. (put)

→ _____ two eggs in the soup.

8 네 티켓들을 가져와라. (bring)

→ _____ your tickets.

9 이 약을 먹어라. (take)

➜ _____ this medicine.

10 두려워하지 마라. (be)

➜ _____ _____ afraid.

11 그들을 위해 음식을 준비하지 마라. (prepare)

➜ _____ _____ the food for them.

12 커피를 너무 많이 마시지 마라. (coffee)

➜ _____

13 여기서 절대로 길을 건너지 마라. (never)

➜ _____

14 샐러드에 후추를 조금 넣어라. (some pepper, salad)

➜ _____

15 너의 코트를 가져와라. (your coat)

➜ _____

16 부끄러워하지 마라. (shy)

➜ _____

17 절대 회의에 다시 늦지 마라. (never, the meeting)

➜ _____

A 다음 단어를 두 번씩 듣고 따라 쓴 후 그 뜻을 쓰세요.

단어	두 번 따라 쓰기		뜻 쓰기
noise 소음			
invite 초대하다			
carefully 주의 깊게			
nap 낮잠			
board game 보드게임			
loudly 큰 소리로			
picnic 소풍			
take care of 돌보다			
express bus 급행 버스			
hide 숨다			
trip 여행			
seatbelt 안전벨트			
ring 울리다			

단어	두 번 따라 쓰기		뜻 쓰기
doorbell 초인종			
forest 숲			
print 인쇄하다			
collect 모으다			
stamp 우표			
performance 공연			
slowly 느리게			
on foot 걸어서			
get on (버스, 기차 등을) 타다			
plant 심다			
water 물을 주다			

A 주어진 철자의 순서를 바르게 맞추어 우리말 뜻에 해당하는 단어를 쓰세요.

1  olctlec
모으다

2  roefts
숲

3  matps
우표

4  etblsaet
안전벨트

5  rnpit
인쇄하다

6  bodorlel
초인종

B 우리말과 같은 뜻이 되도록 보기 에서 알맞은 단어를 골라 쓰세요.

| 보기 | loudly | board game | invite | slowly | water |

1 Let's _____ the garden.   정원에 물을 주자.

2 She didn't _____ us.   그녀는 우리를 초대하지 않았다.

3 This _____ is fun.   이 보드게임은 재미있다.

4 He called me _____.   그가 큰 소리로 나를 불렀다.

5 The turtle moves _____.   그 거북이는 느리게 움직인다.

C 다음 사진에 해당하는 단어를 아래 퍼즐에서 찾아 ○ 표시하고 빈칸에 쓰세요.

s	p	c	l	l	d	w	e	r	q
i	n	o	i	s	e	o	s	o	w
n	a	p	s	t	p	w	e	i	p
a	p	i	r	e	r	h	u	e	l
e	g	c	e	t	r	i	p	o	a
r	i	n	b	d	l	d	u	p	n
b	g	i	o	p	t	e	l	e	t
p	u	c	d	n	q	s	t	l	k

1 낮잠

2 소음

3 숨다

4 여행

5 소풍

6 심다

A ( ) 안에서 알맞은 것을 고르세요.

1 Let's (drink not / not drink) coffee.   커피를 마시지 말자.

2 Shall we (go / going) to the bakery?   우리 빵집에 갈래?

3 What about (wears / wearing) the uniform today?   오늘은 유니폼을 입는 게 어때?

4 (Let's not / Don't let) listen to music loudly.   음악을 크게 듣지 말자.

5 Why don't you (do / doing) your homework?   너 숙제를 하는 게 어때?

6 Let's (turn / turned) off the TV.   TV를 끄자.

7 Why don't we (go / goes) fishing?   우리 낚시를 가는 게 어때?

8 (Not let's / Let's not) take pictures here.   여기서 사진을 찍지 말자.

9 How about (play / playing) chess?   체스를 두는 게 어때?

10 Shall (you / we) paint the door?   우리 문에 페인트칠할래?

11 Let's (clean / cleaning) the room.   방을 청소하자.

12 How about (watch / watching) an action movie?   액션 영화를 보는 게 어때?

B 다음 중 맞는 문장을 고르세요.

1 ⓐ Not let's cross the bridge.　그 다리를 건너지 말자.

　 ⓑ Let's not cross the bridge.

2 ⓐ Why don't we play board games?　우리 보드게임을 하는 게 어때?

　 ⓑ Why don't we playing board games?

3 ⓐ Let's invites Ron to our wedding.　우리의 결혼식에 Ron을 초대하자.

　 ⓑ Let's invite Ron to our wedding.

4 ⓐ Shall we meeting at the airport?　우리 공항에서 만날래?

　 ⓑ Shall we meet at the airport?

5 ⓐ Why you don't write a song?　너 노래를 쓰는 게 어때?

　 ⓑ Why don't you write a song?

6 ⓐ How about play baseball outside?　밖에서 야구를 하는 게 어때?

　 ⓑ How about playing baseball outside?

7 ⓐ Let's make some bread.　빵을 조금 만들자.

　 ⓑ Let's making some bread.

Ⓐ 두 문장이 같은 의미가 되도록 주어진 말을 이용하여 문장을 완성하세요.

1 What about eating out tonight? (Why don't you)   오늘 밤에 외식하는 게 어때?

→ _____ tonight?

2 Let's play soccer. (How about)   축구를 하자.

→ _____ soccer?

3 Shall we drink some juice? (Let's)   우리 주스를 좀 마실래?

→ _____ some juice.

4 How about reading his books? (What about)   그의 책들을 읽는 게 어때?

→ _____ his books?

5 Let's take a taxi. (Shall we)   택시를 타자.

→ _____ a taxi?

6 Why don't we invite Tom to the party? (Let's)   우리 Tom을 파티에 초대하는 게 어때?

→ _____ Tom to the party.

7 How about going to the mall this weekend? (Shall we)
이번 주말에 쇼핑몰에 가는 게 어때?

→ _____ to the mall this weekend?

8 Let's drink green tea. (What about)   녹차를 마시자.

→ _____ green tea?

9 Let's sell those shoes. (Why don't we)   저 신발을 팔자.

→ _____ those shoes?

10 Shall we study together? (How about)   우리 같이 공부할래?

→ _____ together?

B 다음 문장을 주어진 지시대로 바꿔 쓰세요.

1 Don't touch the window. (Let's not 제안문)   창문을 만지지 마라.

→ _____

2 We plant trees today. (What about 제안문)   우리는 오늘 나무들을 심는다.

→ _____

3 Send an email. (Why don't you 제안문)   이메일을 보내라.

→ _____

4 Turn on the music. (Why don't we 제안문)   음악을 틀어라.

→ _____

5 Don't go into the forest. (Let's not 제안문)   숲속으로 들어가지 마라.

→ _____

6 Bring our dog here. (How about 제안문)   우리 개를 여기 데려와라.

→ _____

7 We swim in the pool. (Shall we 제안문)   우리는 수영장에서 수영한다.

→ _____

8 Don't talk about the exam. (Let's not 제안문)   시험에 대해 이야기하지 마라.

→ _____

9 Feed this cat. (Let's 제안문)   이 고양이에게 먹이를 줘라.

→ _____

10 Go to the museum. (Shall we 제안문)   박물관에 가라.

→ _____

A 우리말과 같은 뜻이 되도록 주어진 말을 바르게 배열하세요.

1 물 한 병을 사자. (buy / a bottle of / let's / water / .)

➡ _____

2 이 스웨터를 입는 게 어때? (this sweater / wearing / what / about / ?)

➡ _____

3 공원에서 음식을 먹지 말자. (in the park / not / eat / food / let's / .)

➡ _____

4 너 너의 방학을 즐기는 게 어때? (you / your vacation / why / enjoy / don't / ?)

➡ _____

5 급행 버스를 타자. (an express bus / take / let's / .)

➡ _____

6 우리 낮잠을 자는 게 어때? (why / we / take / don't / a nap / ?)

➡ _____

7 Tina를 위해 인형은 어때? (for Tina / how / a doll / about / ?)

➡ _____

8 우리 이 장미들을 살래? (buy / these roses / we / shall / ?)

➡ _____

9 새 옷을 사는 게 어때? (about / new clothes / what / buying / ?)

➡ _____

10 그 공연을 놓치지 말자. (not / miss / let's / the show / .)

➡ _____

B 밑줄 친 부분을 바르게 고쳐 문장을 다시 쓰세요.

1 How about <u>travel</u> to Busan?   부산으로 여행 가는 게 어때?

➡ _____

2 Why don't we <u>walking</u> slowly?   우리 천천히 걷는 게 어때?

➡ _____

3 Let's <u>throw not</u> the ball.   공을 던지지 말자.

➡ _____

4 Why don't you <u>plans</u> a trip?   너 여행을 계획하는 게 어때?

➡ _____

5 Shall we <u>meeting</u> at 7:00 a.m.?   우리 오전 7시에 만날래?

➡ _____

6 Let's <u>makes</u> a sandcastle together.   같이 모래성을 만들자.

➡ _____

7 What about <u>turn</u> on the TV?   TV를 켜는 게 어때?

➡ _____

8 Why don't we <u>making</u> pasta?   우리 파스타를 만드는 게 어때?

➡ _____

9 <u>Not let's</u> drive too fast.   너무 빨리 운전하지 말자.

➡ _____

10 Shall we <u>orders</u> soda?   우리 탄산음료를 주문할래?

➡ _____

A 우리말과 같은 뜻이 되도록 주어진 말을 이용하여 문장을 완성하세요.

1 교실을 청소하자. (clean)

➡ _____ _____ the classroom.

2 동물들을 괴롭히지 말자. (bother)

➡ _____ _____ _____ the animals.

3 우리 잠시 프랑스에서 지내는 게 어때? (what, stay)

➡ _____ _____ _____ in France for a while?

4 우리 그곳에 걸어서 가는 게 어때? (why, go)

➡ _____ _____ _____ _____ there

on foot?

5 안경을 쓰는 게 어때? (how, wear)

➡ _____ _____ _____ glasses?

6 우리 아침으로 베이글 먹을래? (shall, eat)

➡ _____ _____ _____ bagels for breakfast?

7 너 날짜를 확인하는 게 어때? (why, check)

➡ _____ _____ _____ the date?

8 체육관에 가지 말자. (go)

➡ _____ _____ _____ to the gym.

9 그 부츠를 신어보는 게 어때? (what, try)

➜ _____ _____ _____ on the boots?

10 우리 담요 밑에 숨을래? (shall, hide)

➜ _____ _____ _____ under the blanket?

11 너 다음 주에 돌아오는 게 어때? (why, come)

➜ _____ _____ _____ _____ back

next week?

12 모자를 쓰는 게 어때? (what, a cap)

➜ _____

13 쇼핑몰에 가지 말자. (the mall)

➜ _____

14 다음 달에 돌아오자. (next month)

➜ _____

15 아침으로 시리얼을 먹는 게 어때? (how, cereal)

➜ _____

16 우리 커피를 마실래? (shall, drink coffee)

➜ _____

17 우리 잠시 제주도에서 지내는 게 어때? (why, stay on Jeju-do)

➜ _____